A HACKER'S JOURNEY

Bridges...Between Golf, Wisdom, and Life

Lessons learned from the

"Church of the Fairway" and "Chapel of the Green"

by

Larry Galley

A Hacker's Journey
Bridges...Between Golf, Wisdom, and Life
Lessons learned from the "Church of the Fairway" and "Chapel of the Green"
Author: Larry Galley
Cover and Interior Layout: Michael Nicloy

ISBN-13: 978-1-945907-93-7

Published by Nico 11 Publishing & Design,
Mukwonago, Wisconsin
www.nico11publishing.com

Be well read.

Quantity and wholesale order requests can be emailed to:
mike@nico11publishing.com
or can be made by phone: 217.779.9677

Contact Larry Galley: brdgbldr1@comcast.net

Printed in The United States of America

A Reading Suggestion...

As the one providing the vehicle for the Course you are about to play, I have a suggestion you might wish to consider.

Take your time with this read. If read as the author, yours truly, intended, you will play/read one hole at a time and then take time to <u>process</u> and <u>record</u> your score on the hole just as you would if you were playing in a Saturday match.

There are 18 Holes/Chapters in this book each with its own unique topic. Just as any golf course worth its salt will give you a new opportunity to proceed and tackle the next hole, so too does this writing.

Take your time.

It is my desire that you read, enjoy and perhaps find some personal meaning and potential growth in each hole.

Enjoy. And if inclined to do so share your thoughts with someone you care about.

Enjoy the round.

Contents

Back Nine

By Way of Introduction...

This is not a book of Golf instructions. I have not earned the right to suggest how you should play your game—whether it is golf or life. I can, however, offer you something that you can't get anywhere else. I can offer the experience and learning I have accrued through over 60 years of pursuing the games of golf and life, through their good, bad, and yes, even "ugly moments."

Golf is so much more than "just a game" to me. It has been a wonderful traveling companion through much of my life, providing a significant treasure trove of fond memories and allowed me to experience the beauty, challenges, satisfaction, seasons of growth, and moments of joy I will always cherish. It has also brought me a host of friendships, the learning platform for many of life's crucial lessons, and a haven from a world whose pace of life seems to be ever increasing.

There are very few things I enjoy more than sharing my joy for the game and the things I have learned as a result of it. For a number of years, I have held the belief that golf has a lot to teach us about life if we will just take the time to observe and learn its lessons. I see the game, its aura, the surrounding accouterments, the dynamics, the ever-changing venues, and its expectation of respect, honesty and personal responsibility—all, as rich elements of a conglomerate metaphor for life.

Legendary golfer, Bobby Jones, said "Competitive golf is played mainly on a five and a half inch course ... the space between your ears." In other words, most of the game of golf is about good headwork—WISDOM. I believe life is also a game requiring copious amounts of good headwork and therein, to me, lays the connection between golf and life. It takes WISDOM to fare well in both.

Espousing the belief that Wisdom is a bridge bringing together the adventures of golf and life, it seems logical to me that I ought to seek out the best sources of wisdom to be found and apply those insights to my golf game and to my life. Golf has its books of guidelines and rules for the good of the game. Life also has a book of guidelines I use for the good of my life—it's called scripture, my Bible.

In my seventy-plus years of life, I have never found a more helpful source of wisdom for golf and life than scripture. Golf courses, the game, and its participants have combined to provide me one of God's three-dimensional felt boards illustrating, in living color and experience, the value of biblical scripture.

The beautiful thing about wisdom is that, while it is priceless and many have paid a high price for it, it can be shared ... free of charge. Shared wisdom benefits us all.

Consider the following analogy:

Suppose you and I are each holding a dollar in our hand. We then decide, for whatever reason, to exchange dollars, you give me yours and I give you mine. The net result is that at the end of the transaction we still each have a dollar—no gain.

However, suppose we were to exchange an idea, experience, or story instead of a dollar.

At the end of the transaction, we would both end up with an additional idea, experience, or story in our respective noggins—a 100% gain. To play out the analogy, we can, if we choose, multiply the effects of our learning experience several-fold if we simply choose to share those experiences.

I have a vision ... a vision of an ongoing "Worldwide Golf Story Sharing Group"—I view it as a "Life Group"—sharing golf stories and our learning experiences from the game of golf and how those experiences have contributed to our daily lives. By sharing these experiences—large and small—monumental to minuscule—I see those of us who choose to participate growing significantly in faith, character, integrity, and behavior.

Herein is the simple premise of this effort. When we share we will all be richer for it—no membership, no fees, no rallying cry, just unselfishly share. I know I can't grow you and you can't grow me. I also know, however, we can help one another grow in spirit and in love if we invest ourselves in the process. And, and, and ... we have the opportunity to develop new friends across the world while we're at it. That excites me.

I invite you to join me in this adventure of story sharing, discovery, growth, and joy. You may or may not agree with my conclusions. That's okay. We don't have to agree on everything. In fact, different lenses on a topic are what provide the fertilizer for new or refined understanding. We just need to share.

Fore!

Who is This Guy?

I was born and raised in Battle Creek, Michigan, a rather nondescript little town in south central Michigan, known primarily for the cereal it produces—Kellogg's Corn Flakes. The town enjoyed being, at that time, one of the most visited towns in the state, due to the Kellogg Company factory tours, where families could come and see how corn flakes are made, meet "Tony the Tiger," and have a scoop of vanilla ice cream on a bed of corn flakes to cap off their tour. When the winds were right we, the residents of the town, were treated to the aroma from Kellogg's roasting ovens—a blessing when things were going well, a curse when a batch was overcooked. (This should give you some insight into the excitement level available in my formative years.)

For a good share of my childhood and adolescent years, I spent my spare time looking into the distance and wondering what the bigger world was like and longing to taste it. I didn't realize then, that there was an energetic little rebel spirit kicking, clawing, and pushing to break free from within me to experience that bigger world.

My folks had an inkling that a restless spirit was brewing in my little soul early on when one morning in the midst of my third year of captivity—read life in my little three year olds world—I found a way to break loose from the leather harness and long cord that kept me tethered to the front porch of our house. I was spotted by a concerned neighborhood mother—"the Snitch"—who saw me running buck naked, at flank speed, southbound down North 23rd street, away from our house in route to a destination unknown.

(This was an unfortunate forecast of future behaviors brewing.)

The Snitch immediately called my momma who in turn called the local police thus foiling my intended escape and facilitating my eventual capture by a local constable who placed me in a very large squad car and returned me to my home some twenty minutes later into the hands of an extremely grateful, yet inexplicably (so my little mind thought) angry, momma. While justice was swift in Battle Creek, she was not blind. She had a paddle in her right hand that found the center of my seat several times, providing memories, fresh to this day.

(Warning from the voice of experience: remembering questionable behaviors does not guarantee they will not revisit at some point in the future.)

As a middle schooler and into high school I loved sports—baseball, football, and swimming—and spent most of my summers either on a diamond, playing third base, sweating my tail off in a set of football pads on a practice field, or waterskiing on Goguac Lake. It was also about this time that I started to take an interest in golf … and Girls.

That was life, until my junior year of high school when one day, while visiting my girlfriend's house, her father asked me a couple rather disturbing questions.

"So, Larry, where do you think you will be going to college?" Followed by a momentary pause and then the second question/statement, "You are planning to go to college … aren't you?"

The questions were disturbing to me because until then I had never given College much thought. My thinking went along the lines of…I'll figure that out when the time comes, but hey, that's two years away. Right?

I share all of this now to give you a taste of how absolutely unprepared I was for the bigger life about to come.

At this juncture in my life, I existed in *"run away"* mode, sure that "my own rules" were far better than those anyone else could impose on me. It was also of no consequence to me whether someone might get hurt because of my cavalier stance on life, including myself. Character, honesty, dependability, and responsibility were not yet observable in my persona. I was intent on living in and for the moment. Sadly, anyone was fair game to be used as a player for my convenience in that scenario.

(I want to make clear a sad, but true, point here. I thought I was so slick that I could outwit the system and have everything my own way. That attitude haunts and grieves me to this day.)

I "knew" I could be the center of attention and invisible at the same time. The invisible dimension—so I thought—was so that I could do whatever I wanted, whenever I wanted, with whomever I wanted—assured that no one would know the real me. It never crossed my mind, at the time, that life had purpose and that I was placed here by a power greater than myself for a purpose bigger than myself. You could rightfully say I was a poster boy for self-centeredness.

One could also accurately observe that I jumped into the deep end of the pool of faux (i.e., not quite) adulthood, unprepared for the trauma that my choices and behavior would bring.

Fast-forward seventeen years to the winter of 1982—January to be precise.

I was living—read: existing—in Phoenix, Arizona—having impetuously accepted a work position in Phoenix to *run away* from a job I hated in Chicago. Only to find out upon arrival that the position I was to occupy was in a company on the verge of closing it's doors. What is painfully obvious in this scenario is that I didn't do my *"due diligence."*—Just one of many blunders along the way.

To that point in my life journey, I had graduated high school, married my high school girlfriend, between my sophomore and junior year of college, graduated two years later with a degree in education, fathered a set of twins—a boy and a girl—spent eleven plus years in the U.S. Navy, been to war twice, *run away* from a marriage of seventeen years, leaving a set of now 14-year-old twins behind and found myself pent up in a one-room efficiency apartment facing a rent payment I couldn't make, looking back over an encyclopedia size book of the disastrous decisions I had made since leaving my childhood home in 1965...all the rewards of making my own rules.

It seems redundant to say that I was a mess...but I was a mess!

Having run away from the faith of my upbringing and venturing out with my own set of rules, accepting accountability to no one, not even my wife, I was, at age 37, facing a life so internally desolate I cannot find words adequate to describe it.

Living life by my rules, which were few and far between, had generated such a mess I could see no way to clean it up. Life, to me, appeared hopeless. When I took stock of the situation—to coin a phrase—"I couldn't recognize the guy in the mirror." I had branded myself as a lying, cheating, vagrant runaway. To my recollection, golf was the only bright spot in that miserable montage of experience, but it was not enough. It seemed to me that there was only one option available to ease the pain.

Sitting alone in my nasty little efficiency apartment in Arizona, nursing my wounds and feeling miserably sorry for myself, I made a foolish and extremely selfish decision ... I decided to quit and end my life... in essence, *run away* forever!

To give some insight as to how messed up my thinking really was, I felt it only appropriate to call the man who had always been an inspiration in my life... my Dad. It was his service and patriotism as a Navy man during World War II that had inspired me to join the U.S. Navy during the Vietnam Conflict. Silly as it sounds today, I thought it only right to call and share with him my situation, my decision, and to tell him a final "I love you" and "goodbye."

I placed the battered old dial phone on the arm of the only chair in that abysmal apartment and spun the numbers on the dial to reach him at his office in Michigan. What happened next, I can only attribute to "Divine" intervention.

After a brief "hello", I summoned the courage to share my decision and say goodbye. But when I opened my mouth to speak, the words that came tumbling out were not, "I love you and goodbye." But, instead, the words that came out were:

"I'm in trouble, real trouble—*pause*—can you come?"

From receiving my call in Michigan, interrupting his regular business routine, with no idea that he would be traveling that day, he was by my side in Arizona in less than twelve hours. Talk about a demonstration of unconditional love. I'm the kid who for the past 17 years had been the black sheep of the family and more than once had been a painful disappointment. And yet with only momentary notice, one question, and no explanation, he "set sail" immediately to be by my side as quickly as he possibly could. I asked, "Can you come?" His response? He came! At that moment… he modeled Jesus to me.

(I was functioning under the erroneous assumption that because of my errant life, no one would or could love me. My Dad irrevocably exposed that lie in my thinking by his very presence, without having to say a word.

The bottom…

Words cannot express, for positive reasons this time, how relieved and reassured I was to have someone, whom I knew loved me, by my side to hug and hang on to for even a moment.

During our three days together—which were all too brief—we had multiple opportunities to drive out into the desert and view the majesty of God's creation in its unblemished splendor. During one of those junkets, we pulled off to the side of the road to admire the view and chat. In the midst of our conversation, I started to make a comment that I prefaced with:

"Pop, I know you can't love or respect me but …"

At which point I was abruptly interrupted—a behavior my Dad seldom exhibited—as he said:

"Wait a minute! What gives you the right to tell me who I love or respect? Let's be perfectly clear. I love you. And I respect you…I don't respect your behavior!"

Never, before or since, in my entire life, have I experienced a message so succinct, direct, and on point regarding my life. That message was the pivot point in my life, generating a desire that exists to this day that my behavior be respectable and my demeanor loving and lovable.

I would love to tell you that the interlude I just described with my Dad changed everything, and all for the better. That would be misleading. I had jettisoned any notion that ending my life was the appropriate answer to my challenges. I did, however, still have the substantial mess I had made of my life to clean up.

The Cleanup...

There are no easy solutions or magic potions that one can apply to roughly two decades of disrepair. Some of the pain will last a lifetime even though forgiven. How do you reconcile abandonment, infidelity, carelessness, self-centeredness and the imbedded refrain..."Dad, you left me"?

In all honesty, some days were good, some were not so good, and some were horrible. But one thing had permanently changed. I now had clear verifiable knowledge that I was cared for and loved. With that knowledge as a comfort I have, since my "dance with the darkness," spent significant time learning from, and cleaning up, the mess I had made.

I returned to Chicago from Phoenix in March of the same year, to address the floundering relationship I had created with my spouse due to my mental and moral weakness. (I had trampled on most, if not all, of the moral directives with which I was raised—i.e. the "10 Commandments." Quite predictably, our marriage did not survive the early 80's.

Shortly after my return from Arizona in 1983 I began to study for entry into the Financial Services industry as a Stock Broker. I earned my Securities and Insurance Licenses and in 1984 took a position with E.F. Hutton, a position I held for the next ten years.

Some lessons are harder to learn than others.

In the spring of 1984 I married for a second time. During that same period I worked diligently to mend the shattered relationships I had created with my twins. My professional life as a Stock Broker progressed nicely but our marriage floundered and we finally dissolved the marriage, after eleven years of struggle, due to irreconcilable differences.

It was during this same extended period of confusion or "state of flux" and self reflection that it became obvious to me that *I was a major part of the problems I seemed to continue to face.* But "what to do" was the question.

For me, the first step was...I had to quit *running away!*

Second, I had to resolve that I would do my best to stay on course regardless of the pain that might accompany the process, knowing that this recovery process was likely going to take the rest of my life. I have come to the bedrock understanding that if I want a relationship with my family it will always be my turn to reach out and offer the hand of love regardless of the response…I refuse to give up and *run away* again.

Third, I had to come to grips with the fact that I cannot change or replace the past. I can, however, construct a more savory and God honoring future.

In the mid 90's I exited the Financial Services Industry to enter the Training world. It was during this career transition I enlisted the assistance of a Business Colleague and together, combining her experience in the area of Corporate Training and Development and my Navy background in Leadership and Management, we partnered to create a training enterprise under the name "Bridge Builders" to help corporations and organizations refine their leadership and communication skills.

The great news for me is that on August 13, 2004, that same "Business Colleague" became my wife and as of this writing we have been in partnership 27 years and are now in the midst of our 17th year of marriage. She is an ongoing blessing and rudder for my life.

In addition, in the mid 90"s, I had a beautiful encounter with my Maker that irrevocably altered my life's heading in the direction of eternal success and well-being with Him. Today, my scarred and mangled life is without blemish in His eyes. For me it can't get any better than that.

(A cautionary note from a voice of experience: One of the more difficult realities I have had to come to grips with in my clean-up process is this: One can request and receive forgiveness. It is unrealistic and inadvisable, however, to expect "forget-ness." Not only is it unrealistic, but it is also very likely unhealthy for all involved.)

In retrospect, I find it endearing that God, in his infinite wisdom, knew that I was not going to voluntarily pick up and study the guidance he had so graciously provided in his scriptures—guidance that has stood the test of time over literally thousands of years. He knew I had neither the patience nor the interest in pursuing things that might be of greater importance than myself at the moment. So with gentleness, caring, purpose, and love, He introduced me to the beauty and grandeur of His creation through the golf course.

During this extended time of reparations and life changes, I have found great solace and peace in the restorative qualities of golf, both the game and the venues surrounding the game.

God allowed me to learn—experientially—the need for rules, respect, love, self-control, and the inextricable link between behaviors and consequences. It was in this setting that I began to understand and embrace the fact that I alone am responsible for my behaviors and the consequences that ensue—whether positive or negative.

It was there, on the golf course that my whole perspective on life and appreciation for rules began to change. I began to recognize—as psychologist and author Henry Cloud puts it, *"Rules are not made to be broken ... they are made to keep us from being broken."* I began to absorb the fact that rules were not intended to limit me, but to help me survive, thrive, and derive the joy that can accrue in our complicated and somewhat tortured world, both on the golf course and on the larger stage of life.

From a position of callous consumption and self-centeredness, my heart has been transformed to one of appreciation and thankfulness for the gifts I have been given. For years I joked with my playing buddies that I attended the "church of the fairway" and the "chapel of the green." Little did I realize that this was not a joke, it was my reality. God, who met me where I was, has been, and continues to be, graciously good to me.

A Starter Sampler ...

Here are just some of the realizations that have come my way over the years from the golf course and its surroundings:

- Life is a gift to enjoy, not merely endure.

- There is beauty to be found in the strangest places.

- Life is better when shared in community than having to go it alone—Foursomes are often more fun than playing alone.

- Fairness can be pleasing to the soul—I have found it pleasing to excel while playing within the bounds of the rules.

- Beauty without maintenance leads to burnout—Maintenance is an essential ingredient of longevity. A beautifully designed golf course only stays beautiful when it is beautifully maintained. The same can be said for my life.

- Planning trumps passion. Did you ever get to the golf course only to find that you had been in such a hurry to get there you left your clubs at home?

- To ignore warnings and caution signs is to court disaster.

- There is great beauty in simplicity.

- Being informed is far better than operating on the fly.

- Always come equipped to play—physically, emotionally, and spiritually.

- Attitude impacts behavior and hence results. Scanning my attitude daily is a must!

- Good results come out of good practice.

- Paying attention to the details can lower your score. It can also improve, or even save, your life.

- Courtesy is never out of line—Love your neighbor is always in play.

- I play better and enjoy myself more when I am relaxed. Patience helps me relax—patience takes practice.

- My expectations have a lot to do with my performance—Expectations need a reality check.

- My performance is fueled by the gifts God has given me.

Today ...

Having used the golf course as my starter kit to appreciating a good life, I have graduated from "wrestling with" to "welcoming" the rules and guidance set down in Gods scripture that have no expiration date. I have never enjoyed playing by the rules "because I have to." But my perspective on who rules my life is significantly different today. I have God's rules embedded in my heart to follow, not because I have to, but "because I want to." My desire is to delight my Maker as a way of saying "thank you" for the life and purpose he has given me.

For over half of a century, the golf course and the game have functioned as exquisite facilitators of learning in my life. Within these pages, I have tried to share some of the revelations God has provided me from my golfing experience. What you do with that sharing is entirely up to you. It is my hope that my sharing will, in some way, infuse your game and your life with additional joy—a few aha moments—and perhaps help shape some of your thinking for your future good.

Remember: In golf and in life there are no do-overs ... only grace, forgiveness, and the opportunity to take another shot until you finish the round.

Hit 'em straight and enjoy the round.

L.G.

Keeping Score

Golf and life are both demanding games. To play them well, and to have our scores count, a scorecard is kept to record the outcome of each hole or event in our lives.

We keep a scorecard, not only to give others an honest appraisal of our current performance but also to provide ourselves with honest feedback as to what is working well and what might need improvement at any given time.

Scorecard

	1	2	3	4	5	6	7	8	9	Out	Total
Par	5	4	4	3	4	4	3	5	4	36	
Yardage	547	409	320	295	363	333	278	454	378	3377	
Score											

	10	11	12	13	14	15	16	17	18	In	Total
Par	5	4	3	4	4	5	4	4	3	36	
Yardage	498	344	228	329	357	436	340	393	285	3210	6587
Score											

Final Score ☐

At the end of each of the eighteen holes you are about to experience, you will find a scorecard to assess your current performance in the area addressed on that hole. Just as you would not move on to the next hole on your Saturday match without tallying your score, be sure to take a little time to provide yourself a personal assessment of how you feel you have done, or are doing, so far in each of the 18 holes.

Hole #1

Par 5

547 Yards

The Master Chief, the Tee, and Me ...
... a Mentor in Action

(Mentoring)

To this day I can vividly remember over fifty plus years ago—the spring of 1970 to be precise—walking together with him onto the first tee. We were getting ready to tee it up for our first round of golf at Naval Air Station (NAS) Barbers Point Golf Course, on the Island of Oahu in the state of Hawaii, located just a short distance across the water from the Arizona Memorial, dedicated to the Sailors, Marines, Airmen, and Soldiers who lost their lives in the infamous attack on Pearl Harbor on December 7, 1941. His name was Jack Adams and he was, by profession, a Master Chief Petty Officer in the United States Navy.

As he was pulling on his golf glove over his big left hand he looked at me—with a wide smile, showing a whole mouth full of perfectly formed brilliantly white teeth that a toothpaste company would have been proud to put in their ads—and said, "Well, are you ready?"

I responded, "Yup."

He just chuckled. It was then that I realized I didn't know what he was really asking me. Of course, he was asking me if I was ready to tee it up, ready to play.

Right? Or was he?

All of a sudden I wasn't sure. So, thinking I was being funny, I turned to him and glibly asked, "By your question, 'Are you ready?' did you mean ready to play, ready to get beat, ready for life, ready for eternity, ready for what?"

He just chuckled again and said, "Yup."

With that he bent over, placed his tee in the ground, fiddled with his ball for a moment to ensure it was setting on the tee just right, stood back, took his stance over the ball and proceeded to hit his first shot straight down the middle of the fairway.

With one seemingly simple question—"are you ready?"—he had challenged me to think for the present, for the future, about things mundane to things of eternal significance, and everything in between. School in the hands of the Master Chief had truly begun.

In retrospect, his soft chuckle said, "Son, you have much to learn. I'll walk with you and help you get your sea legs. I'll gladly ask the questions. But you need to understand right from the start that you are going to have to do the thinking, the soul-searching and yes, the praying for the answers."

We laughed, I hit my tee shot, and we moved off down the fairway into a relationship that I have cherished for decades.

I first met the Master Chief while I was a U.S. Navy Lieutenant assigned to Navy Patrol Squadron VP 1, home ported at NAS Barbers Point, Hawaii. At that time he, the Master Chief, had recently joined our squadron as Master Chief Petty Officer of the Command (MCPOC). For the uninitiated, his title, MCPOC, designated him the number one enlisted man in the squadron and as such he was responsible for the performance, care, feeding and well being of all three hundred and some enlisted personnel in our squadron.

By comparison, I was a still-wet-behind-the-ears junior officer responsible for the leadership of twelve people assigned to one of the squadron maintenance branch offices. At the time of our meeting he had over thirty years of experience under his belt, I had three.

One day, shortly after his arrival in the squadron, the Master Chief saw me walking down one of the passageways in the hangar area and called out to me: "Mr. Galley ... Lieutenant ... Sir, can we talk a minute?"

I said, "Sure, Master Chief, what's up?"

He walked up to me and gently put his hand on my shoulder, looked down at me—*the Master Chief was six foot four... I am not*—and graciously motioned toward a side passageway to a more private location with his free hand gesturing as if to say "Please, step into my office."

Lesson One: To earn "respect" you must " show respect."

Now, you need to understand something about Master Chief Adams. He wasn't your ordinary, run of the mill, garden variety Master Chief. This was a man with a whole sleeve full of gold hash marks or gold stripes displayed on his uniform, signifying over thirty years of exemplary service to the United States Navy.

So much was he respected throughout the Navy community, that he was one of the top ten finalists under consideration to assume the assignment as number one enlisted man in the entire U.S. Navy, a role that would carry the title Master Chief Petty Officer of the Navy (MCPON).

His reputation had preceded him and while I outranked him, he being an enlisted man and I an officer, I was in awe of him and admired him for what he had been able to accomplish throughout his career. When he spoke even the Commanding Officer listened. And now it was my turn to listen.

As we walked slowly down the passageway (hallway), his hand gently resting on my shoulder to guide me along, he began to talk: "Mr. Galley, Sir," he said, "I really like you. You're going to make a great officer *someday.*" *(Notice he didn't say, "you really are a great officer" – LG)*

Cautiously I responded, waiting for the other shoe to drop: *"Yeeaah."*

There was a short pause and then he continued: "But Sir, *(another slight pause accompanied by a gentle smile)* you've got a lot to learn *(yet another pause and then softly and slowly)* and if you would allow, I would be delighted to help you in that process."

Fortunately, for me, the good Lord gave me the common sense to say, "I would appreciate that very much, Master Chief."

And just that fast, with a gentleness and finesse I will always remember, he inserted himself into my life. He took an interest in me and began to offer up his own private college of knowledge, gained through many years of service to his country and his shipmates. He was unstinting in passing on the lessons he had learned.

He became my "sea daddy," my mentor. Somehow he saw in me a teacher in the making. He took me under his wing and taught me the ways of good management and leadership, not from what he had read in books but from the volumes in his own library of experience, both good and bad. He cared about me, invested in me, and shared his best with me. Not because he had to, but because he wanted to.

Lesson Two: Extend yourself—offer your input and do it in a gentle and respectful manner...

He intimated—without saying aloud—"Learn from my example. I'm going to teach you how to share with people in a way they will remember, learn, and act upon."

Through some good-natured bantering, he found we had a mutual interest—a common ground—in golf. Neither of us played like professionals but we both loved the game. With that information, the die was cast. He had found the setting he needed to work with me, one on one.

Lesson Three: Go where they are...escort them to new understandings...

The setting was pleasant yet challenging, which would give him ample stimuli from which to craft his points. So we agreed to meet later in the week, at the NAS Barbers Point Golf Course, for a sunset round, after work. The golf course became our classroom. He had been granted permission to proceed and he wasted no time in getting started. The lessons intensified during our very first round.

Lesson Four: "You gotta know the course"...

The first time we played the air station golf course was his first time to play the course since transferring into our squadron. As we made our way down the fairway after our first shots he asked, "Have you played this course much?"

I responded rather nonchalantly: "A few times."

A moment or so later he asked, "Any big trouble on this hole?"

I paused for a moment or two to search for some tidbit of knowledge that might be of some importance—remember: the Master Chief had a good thirty years more life experience at his disposal than did I. Then, in an authoritative voice, intended to invoke confidence in my credibility I offered, "No, as a matter of fact, this is not a particularly difficult course to navigate. Probably the biggest hazard on the course is the coral just beneath the turf in the fairways. If you're not careful you can really mess up a club."

He offered a quick "thanks" and was off to hit his second shot and I to mine.

When we came back together on the green he said, "You seem to know this course pretty well."

My reply at the time rings with a touch of naiveté and braggadocio as I look back on it today. I remember saying, "Yeah, well, if you are going to score well, you gotta know the course."

He gave a nod of the head and a small sigh and muttered, "Ain't that the truth."

We played on for several holes sharing pleasantries and laughing as we went. Then, seemingly out of the blue, as if the idea had just struck him, he went back to the conversation we had been having on the first hole. It was as if no time had elapsed between sentences. He made direct eye contact with me and in a quiet, quizzical voice and a raised eyebrow, which suggested that this was a subject that had troubled him for some time; he asked…"Do you really think that's true?"

Somewhat puzzled as to what he might be thinking, and not sure what he was referencing, I responded, "Is 'what' true, Master Chief?"

He responded quickly with "Well sir, back in the #1 fairway you said, 'In order to score well, you gotta know the course.' Right?"

"Right," I said.

Whereupon he pressed the point: "Do you really think that's true?"

Convinced that I was on solid ground, I shot back, without batting an eye: "Absolutely! What makes you ask?"

With that he came back with a soft qualifier to my firm position: "Well, Sir, I was just thinking about that comment and how, even on a course as simple as this, there are probably a number of subtle nuances we need to take into account. Right?"

My immediate response, not wanting to appear overconfident or uninformed of the potential pitfalls that might lie ahead, was "Oh sure there are."

"I thought so," he said, and we continued on.

Note: Please observe the deftness and caring the Master Chief exhibited as he planted the seeds of wisdom he wanted to see grow in me.

Further on in our round, somewhere on the backside, he once again looked at me and asked, like it was still bothering him: "You don't suppose that 'gotta know the course' stuff applies to life like it does to the golf course, do ya?"

I immediately replied, "Of course it does. We always have to be paying attention to what lies ahead. That's why we have navigation charts to get the lay of the land and pre-flight briefings prior to takeoff so that we can get some idea of what to expect."

I was feeling pretty good now because I was really helping the Master Chief out with some issues that were obviously bothering him. (Can you feel the hook being set to reel me in to a new level of understanding?)

After a moment's pause he said, "You know, not to belabor a point but, I'll bet, based on what you have said Sir, about this 'need to know stuff', you think it's important that you know the people you are responsible for every bit as well as you know the characteristics of the golf course you are about to play. I mean you feel you need to know the subtle nuances of each individual you work with to get the best result for all involved. Am I correct?"

While I hadn't thought of my people in quite that light, I wasn't about to appear ignorant in the eyes of the Master Chief so I said in a voice a little less sure than before, "Of course."

Seeds Planted!

Now I was the one looking a little confused and bewildered. The Master Chief hadn't done anything to upset my game. In fact, we had a delightful time, which was now coming to an end as we reached the eighteenth green. My consternation was in the fact that he had scratched the surface of an area I had never really seriously considered being important.

I understood the value of structure, had a working knowledge of the rules, and was well informed on the proper chain of command. But what the Master

Chief had deftly pointed out to me was that I was drastically lacking in one of the most important aspects of leadership.

I needed to be paying attention to the individuality—the subtle nuances—of each of the people assigned to me, which should, if I was leading well, dictate my behaviors with each of them as individuals and how I lead my group.

As we putted out and walked off the last green I felt somewhat sheepish and foolish while at the same time invigorated that this man had intentionally extended himself and chosen to begin to share some of the insights that had made him so successful.

While we were putting our clubs in our cars and changing shoes to go our separate ways he looked at me and said, "Mr. Galley, would you mind if I leave you with just a couple questions to ponder?"

I heard my mouth say, "Of course not, Master Chief."

At the same time, my insides were bracing for the onslaught of intellectual stupidity or nakedness I was sure I would feel from this obviously much more experienced man.

"I gotta ask ya, Mr. Galley, (pause) Sir ... how well do you know your people?" *(Read, how well do you know and understand the subtle nuances of each person you are attempting to lead?).* "Give it some thought, Sir. "

He let me think about his question for a moment and then said, "Here are some things I would encourage you to consider. Ask yourself: is it important for me to know my people like I know a golf course? If you believe, as I do, that it is, then ... why is that? How well do I really know my people at present? What do I think the benefits might be to all concerned if I knew my people a little better? How can I get to know them better, and they me?"

Then, with a gentle pat on the back, he warmly shook my hand, making eye contact with me as if to say, "I know I've given you a lot to think about, right out of the chute but I'm confidant you can handle it."

He turned to get in his car and then turned back just long enough to say, "Give it some thought, Sir, just give it some thought."

And with that, he got in his car and drove off, leaving me to process what we had shared.

Lesson Five: Good leadership is a journey, not a destination...

That wasn't so bad. He didn't lecture, belittle, or berate me for my naiveté. He did challenge me to take what I already knew in one part of my life—the golf course—and begin the act of transposing that understanding to other facets of my life as well. In essence, he was saying "You don't have to start from scratch, use what you know and grow from there. You can use the golf course as a baseline from which to grow. Now, think through what we shared."

Lesson Six: Good "leaders" invest themselves in the growth of those they are leading...

For the next two and a half years he invested in me via the golf course and I ate it up. I loved it. I was the student. He was the mentor. Through years of experience, trial and error, in working with young people such as myself, he knew that it would never work to sit in an office and calmly say, "O.K. listen up young man, I have many important lessons in life and leadership for you to learn, so take notes. You will be tested."

Lesson Seven: If you want to truly communicate, seek a level playing field

Casually, the Master Chief looked for a level playing field where we could share comfortably, in-depth and without interruption. It had to be a place where we could take off the rank and positional differences, which defined our professional roles, and allow us to communicate eye to eye, simply as one human being caring about another.

Lesson Eight: It isn't about shouting … it's about sharing…

He seemed to have a never-ending stream of ideas and suggestions as to what I might want to think about and possibly incorporate in my leadership/ life style. He was constantly encouraging me to lead by example embracing the reality that "my people" would be watching me in every facet of my life, not just during the time I spent at the squadron.

He allowed me to see that my credibility—and hence my ability to lead (i.e., my currency with my people) was always a prize to protect. It wasn't until much later in life that I realized the things he was teaching me were age-old concepts, tried and true core values, biblical directives, passed on through multiple millennia.

At least once a week we would leave the squadron after operations had secured for the day and go directly to the golf course whereupon class would begin. Sometimes his tutelage would take the form of questions and at others it would come as definitive statements. He deftly used the golf course and its surroundings as a canvas on which to paint the ideas and images he wanted me to emblazon on my mind and heart.

Lesson Nine: Be creative. Use your surroundings to "plant the seeds" to reinforce your sharing…

Whether waiting on the tee, killing time while waiting for a slow foursome in front of us, or simply moving on from one shot to the next, he would use anything his eyes could drink in to help reinforce a point he was trying to share.

He was the one who pointed out and cemented in my mind many of the signposts I see, to this day, every time I play golf. His skill at taking a piece of something I enjoyed so much and turning it into a learning tool was delightful, instructive and now one of the mainstays in my "leadership toolbox."

His thoughts and ideas were shared with laughter, joy, and heartfelt emotion. His comments were pithy, to the point, never preachy. He wasn't worried about authorship, only sharing. He would find a way to weave in one or two meaty ideas per round to think through and process. His observations would run the gamut from a specific point about leadership and how to bring out the best in others to dealing with some "sticky organizational issue."

Lesson Ten: Be prepared and then, let your style and words fit the occasion...

I am convinced that he knew, long before we reached the golf course what he wanted to cover with me each time we met. What I find so delightful, in retrospect, is the manner in which the Master Chief chose to mentor/teach.

He made no distinction between my professional, personal, emotional, or spiritual life. He would simply look around for a catalyst or vehicle on which to launch a question for me to ponder and then gently and sincerely ask a thought-provoking question on the subject he had chosen to share.

He had the confidence in me to know that I was sincere in my desire to learn and grow on my life's journey, and as such would think through the questions he was posing. He also knew that if I took the time and energy to reflect and respond to his queries, I would be equipping myself to effectively deal with many of the challenges he was sure lay in my future.

Lesson Eleven: Give them your best ... put your signature on your work...

For the entire time, I enjoyed the Master Chief's mentorship he gave me the very best part of him. More than anything else, I remember his heart. He was always interested in my personal well being and growth. He truly was investing in the future, for the Navy, for me, and, as I later found out, for his Maker. I can only hope he took as much pleasure from his efforts as I did.

It was not until a significant time after we first met that I learned what lay at the core of all the Master Chief had chosen to share with me. He had a deep-seated belief in God and the leadership teachings he adhered to and shared that were found in his Bible.

(It is important to note that at that particular juncture in my life, I was not a consciously committed believer. So while his sharing came straight from the core teachings of scripture, he shared them more as generally accepted foundational footings of solid leadership.)

Starting with the simple premise of "Mr. Galley, you have a lot to learn," and an understanding that "people learn best that which they discover for themselves," he dedicated himself to the process of creating learning opportunities and then allowed me the privilege of discovering what he wanted me to learn. He was not flashy, arrogant, or pushy in sharing his thoughts with me. Rather he consistently followed a model of sharing for which I am profoundly thankful to this day. The model he used was simple and straightforward. He found it in his Bible:

"Quietly trust yourself to Christ your Lord and if anybody asks you why you believe as you do, be ready to tell them, and do it in a gentle and respectful manner." (1 Peter 3:15, NLT)

In looking back on my experience with the Master Chief I find myself in awe of the kindness and sense of humor of God. He sent a messenger just for me and gave that messenger the insight to know that the best way to reach me was through a golf course. He entrusted me to the hands of the Master Chief until such time as I was ready to come willingly to a firsthand relationship with the Master of the Master Chief. I will forever be thankful to God and the Master Chief for sharing with such clarity those footings that I now embrace as life principles that I needed to learn.

I thank God for the gift of Master Chief Petty Officer, Jack Adams, USN.

The wisdom that comes from heaven is first of all pure and of quiet gentleness. Then it is peace loving and courteous. It allows discussion and is willing to yield to others: it is full of mercy and good deeds. It is whole hearted straightforward and sincere.
   – James 3:17 (NLT)

Work for the Practice Range:

◄ Do you a have a "Sea Daddy" (Mentor) or two in your life? (If so, please write their names below.)

◄ What caused you to allow them to mentor you?

◄ Reflect for a few moments and then write down what are some of the **key lessons** you have learned from them.

◄ Are you currently anyone else's Sea Daddy/Mentor—in addition to your offspring? If so, please write their names below.

◄ Are you willing to mentor if the possibility presents itself? Y/N

◄ If you are willing to be a mentor, have you made your willingness to mentor known?

How would you score yourself in the area of ***Mentoring?***

(Scale: Quite well … Birdie 4; Okay … Par 5; Needs work … Bogey 6; A disaster … Double Bogey 7)

Scorecard

	1	2	3	4	5	6	7	8	9	Out	Total
Par	5	4	4	3	4	4	3	5	4	36	
Yardage	547	409	320	295	363	333	278	454	378	3377	
Score											

	10	11	12	13	14	15	16	17	18	In	
Par	5	4	3	4	4	5	4	4	3	36	
Yardage	498	344	228	329	357	436	340	393	285	3210	6587
Score											

Notes:

Hole #2

Par 4

409 Yards

Whatchu Waitin' For?

(Fear and Mind Games)

Some years ago we purchased a new set of golf clubs for one of the members of our small traveling golf entourage. They stand in their bag in the garage, ready for their next trip to the links. These are proud clubs, all shiny and bright, custom fitted with special shafts, residing in a padded bag replete with balls, gloves, tees, and all the stuff so essential to playing a great game of golf.

They have been on courses from the tip of Baja in Mexico to the shores of Puget Sound in Washington State. They have toured from the Atlantic and Pacific coasts and innumerable stops in between. With every visit, they have witnessed the unique beauty that can be attained when God and man cooperate to create a wonderful golf course.

These clubs have been up close and personal with tees, fairways, bunkers, water hazards, and greens on a multitude of golf courses. They have heard many lessons about the cooperative team spirit required between head, shoulders, arms, hands, hips, legs, feet, and club to function as equal partners in executing a well-crafted shot.

Each club has been designed precisely to perform a specific function. And each club is available to be called into action to perform feats well beyond its design. Every club stands ready to enter the game, without hesitation, to go wherever, whenever called upon to do the bidding of their master. They stand continually strong and erect in their bag, a perfect complement to the surroundings they have visited.

These warrior clubs are filled with desire to do battle for their master. They all long to feel the exhilaration of shot by shot, conquering the foe. They are eager to experience the satisfaction of a shot well struck, ball flying straight and true to its mark—settling gently onto the green and coming to rest next to the pin. They gleefully anticipate the accolades for a well-executed shot. What joy! What pride!

Alas, in the years these clubs have accompanied us, not once have they come out of the bag to drive a ball off the tee down the fairway, into the water or rough, into a bunker or onto a green. They have attempted no approach shots or putts that rim the cup. They still reside comfortably in their bag, brand new, not a pebble scratch on them. They have had ample opportunities for lessons and practice, yet not one swing in a game. They have become the touring clubs—seeing lots of courses, but never any action.

I'm sure that—could those clubs speak—they would say things like, "Come on, I can do it. Use me! Let me work my magic! What are you afraid of?"

At this point, you might be saying, "Wait a minute. That's ridiculous! Put those clubs to work. It's just a simple exercise in applied physics—nothing more and nothing less. You take an inert object—a golf ball—mount it on another inert object—a tee. Then through a process of energy transfer, accomplished by application of an energy transfer tool—a golf club—trigger the launching of your ball in the direction you have intended. What's so hard about that?"

Of course, there are a few essential variables that need attention when executing a golf club swing including the position of your hands on the club, position of the club head, angle of attack, pitch, and club head path—that will dictate the direction in which the ball will travel. The velocity of the energy transfer will determine the distance the ball will travel: The slower the club head velocity at impact, the shorter the ball will travel. Conversely, the faster the club head is traveling at impact, the farther the ball will go.

Once you understand these few basic principles you simply add to the mix the fact that the golf ball and the golf club are without intelligence and rely entirely upon you for guidance. You are the boss. You are in charge. You decide how much playing time each club will receive. Your golf club and ball will always respond instantly and without reservation to your directions. You are in control. How much better can it get?

Right?

Well ... yes, but ... to get a more accurate and complete picture of the golf club swing we must add the human component. No two of us are exactly alike. We each have a unique golf swing—one that we ourselves have crafted. When we chisel out a golf swing, a starter list of suggested relevant sub-components includes desire, a modicum of knowledge, planning, preparation, emotion, controlled energy, coordination, and timing. And over time, patience, practice, and perseverance will also join the list.

It is this list of human components that makes golf so personally challenging and enjoyable for some and so intimidating to others. In these and many other respects, I find golf to be a wonderful metaphor of life. The truth is that the games of golf and life are willful processes. Nothing will occur just by knowing or thinking about what to do. It takes defined, dedicated, directed action.

Golf requires the development of many skill sets that are foreign to the player. Learning them seems overwhelming to some and to others just part of the process. Regardless, the learning process cannot be "microwaved." It is a process that takes time and is frequently messy. Ongoing challenges litter the pathway. And, because of our human nature, the learning process is frequently marred by setbacks and slumps, both physical and emotional. Golf is no different from anything else at which we want to excel. *Success without mess is highly unlikely.*

The fears that keep many of us sitting at the edge of the tee box of life and watching others enjoy themselves have their taproots embedded in pain avoidance. We just don't want to pay the price of experiencing the mess and the pain we anticipate will accompany us on our learning journey.

Many of us would gladly get into the game of life in the arena of our choosing, if we could just twitch our nose and immediately have the swing and mind of an accomplished golfer, the healing skills of a doctor, or the heart and soul of a minister. Ohhh, to have the ability of a writer to paint verbal pictures, the ability of a musician to combine sight, sound and smell into notes, or whatever else you could imagine! You name it. It's messy long before it's magnificent!

Life has taught me, however, overnight successes aren't overnight. I have had to accept the fact that, as Zig Ziglar put it, "The elevator to the top is broken"; I am going to have to take it one step at a time."[1] I too must slog through the swamp of learning to ascend the stairs of success in any given endeavor. There is no way around the swamp and all of its creepy-crawly unknowns. Each time I step out into areas of uncertainty, my mind screams, "Here comes the pain!"

A confession...

I cannot feel the pain of your experiences; no one can but you. I can, however, describe my own struggle with pain avoidance. Some 20 years ago, I started scribbling notes to myself about the parallels between golf and life. After ten years and the accrual of a mountain of notes, observations and ideas I started to arrange that mountain into a sequence that seemed to make sense, with the idea that perhaps I would write a book—"someday."

Over the years I have told many people about these ideas and how I might become an author. I was pleasantly surprised that many were enthusiastic and supportive. Some even said they wanted to read what I wrote when it was published. Such positive comments were a real rush to my ego. Then, I started testing the market and got positive feedback saying, "Go for it." That began more than ten years ago.

---

1   Zig Ziglar, *See You at the Top*, Pelican Publishing, Co. 2nd Revised edition, 2003, (Pg. 32)

What has taken so long? What has been the problem?

The simple answer is that the same ego that was so bolstered by all of the positive comments could not stand the idea of possibly underperforming. I feared many people would be disappointed in my work. I was driven, or in this case hindered, not by my vision or by the tugs at my soul, but my pride/ego and the fear of my failure. To those who urged me to go for it, I was not willing to admit that I had been stalling to "get good" in private. How could I possibly tell them that I was afraid? They might think less of me once they had read my work.

I dreaded the potential for public ridicule that might come, were I to share the contents of my private library of thoughts.

What if people didn't agree with what I wrote? What if they didn't like what I wrote? And, most important to me, what if the reader found nothing relevant in what I shared? I would be irrelevant! I would be on display! People would see my intellectual nakedness, or, that I talked a better game than I played. I would appear stupid and be dismissed.

(Just as an aside: You wouldn't happen to have a few obstructionist gremlins of your own hiding in your emotional closet would you?)

My rationale—some of it conscious and some subconscious—went like this...

If I don't finish the writing, but simply keep my thoughts in note form, my work will never be published. If I don't take my work to a publisher, I will not have to face the possibility and pain of being rejected. If I don't publish, you can't challenge my ideas. If I don't publish, I don't have to endure your constructive criticism, which won't be constructive. If I don't publish, you can't provide your spin on my ideas. They remain my ideas packed snugly—or should it be smugly—away in my writer's notebook.

To my discredit as a supposed rational thinker, I did not have a speck of evidence to support the validity of my fears. I spent so much time installing the bars on my little gremlins closet that I lost sight of the fact that the ideas I feared sharing weren't even mine. I had encountered them while studying in my Maker's presence. They were His ideas, revealed to me on the church of the fairway and the chapel on the green. My proprietary attitude and pride of authorship were at best inappropriate.

At this point, an idea, new to me, was beginning to burn in my soul. Emotional pain is a guaranteed by-product of participating in the games of golf and of life.

Prolific author John Ortberg suggests that I can't grow without stretching or stepping out of my comfort zone,[2] which requires that I take some risks and try new things. Risk implies the potential for failure and, indeed, failures do occur. Emotional failure is painful. I had yet to come to grips with the reality that while emotional failure may be painful, it is not terminal. It may in fact be the birth pains of a new and brighter future ... if I get in, or stay in, the game.

What became such a blinding glimpse of the obvious to me was that regardless of the decision I made to either get into the game—write—or sit by the tee box and watch others play—keep my inspiration to myself, I was going to experience at least some pain. What I hadn't carefully considered, however, was that the type of pain I would incur varied greatly, depending upon the decisions I made.

If I chose to sit by the tee box and not get in the game—in this case, the writing game—I could expect the long-term pain of the "coulda, shoulda, woulda's." These are among the saddest, most forlorn messages of the heart. They indicate an ongoing sense of failure, defensiveness, and loss. They are indicators of significant voids created by decisions not to engage. While not necessarily permanent, these voids are painful reminders of a life that could have been. They each have a slightly different slant but they all have the same bottom line message:

"I had an opportunity and I did not take it."

During this time of soul-searching and perplexity, I was challenged to do my own little cost/benefit analysis. I decided to weigh the costs of writing against the benefits and see which outweighed the other. It did not take long for me to realize that choosing not to write was tantamount to possibly missing the greatest adventure of my life.[3]

---

2 John Ortberg, *If You Want To Walk On Water You Gotta Get Out Of The Boat,*

3 Luke 14:28-32

Yes, likely, there would be times when what I produced would not be good enough for publication and yes, I am sure I would not enjoy that sense of frustration from being sent back to the keyboard to refine what I already felt was pretty good. But now a desire was bubbling inside me. The adventure and experience seemed to outweigh the costs.

If I chose to step to the tee and get in the game (write) there would be hard work, frustration, setbacks, and perhaps even some humiliation. But the end result would be a new level of understanding, broader horizons, additional new opportunities and the joy of working in the heart of my passion. When I was finally able to come to a decision to get into the game I was able to encapsulate that decision in three words ... I choose life!

I chose to experience, as sportscaster Jim McKay used to say in his introductory voice-over to ABC's Wide World of Sports, "the thrill of victory and the agony of defeat." I chose to have texture, color, and variety in my life. I wanted to feel my heart pump, not merely to assume that it was at rest, buried somewhere deep in my chest.

Freedom...

I believe my decision to step to the tee and get in the game was a wise one. Before I was able to begin, however, I had to respond to the question:

"Who are you trying to please?"

The answer to that question did not come easily. It took much soul-searching and introspection to come to the heartfelt realization that who I really wanted was to delight my Maker.

To delight Him meant I needed to listen to the tugs coming from within and respond positively to them. Or, to put it in the words of my wife Suzanne: "You need to clear your mind, clear your ego, listen to God and do/write what He opens your heart to. To function otherwise would be to try to perform just to feed your ego."

Given the choice of obey or perform, I chose to obey and in the process have experienced the lifting of a tremendous emotional load from my shoulders. I did not know how much more at peace I would be until I started the process of letting go of my need to perform and replacing it with my willingness to respond to the tugs of my soul. When I did respond to those tugs a simple message began to resonate within me:

"Trust me. We have some sculpting to do. We have shaping: molding, scraping, and sanding that must be done. And yes, there will be some pain along the way, but I will be with you every step of the way and I guarantee you, 'I have a plan for you. It is a plan for good and not for evil, to give you a future and a hope.'[4] Just trust me."

I am only beginning to realize how fulfilling and exciting life in the fairway with the Master can be. I don't feel locked in my self-constructed little closet of gremlins anymore. My fears have abated. I feel less stress and I am able to think more clearly. I remember again that I was put on this earth to love, not necessarily impress, others. I cannot impress God, but I can delight Him and love Him through my willingness to listen to and follow the tugs of my soul.

I am a treasured child of the Most High God. He made me perfect for his perfect plan for me. What I have learned is that *fear exists in the absence of confidence of the end result.* I no longer have to worry about the end result—that's God's job. My job is simply to obey, not try to impress. I don't have to prove anything to anyone anymore.[5] I am free!

"Consult not your fears but your hopes and your dreams. Think not about your frustrations, but your unfulfilled potential. Concern yourself not with what you have tried and failed in, but with what it is still possible for you to do."

Pope John XXIII[6]

---

4   Jeremiah 29:11

5   Mark 8:35

6   ¹ ThinkExist.com Quotations. "Pope John XXIII quotes". <u>ThinkExist.com Quotations</u> <u>Online</u> 1 Sep. 2007. 31 Oct. 2007 <http://einstein/quotes/Pope_John_XXIII/>

Work for the Practice Range:

◄ Are you "sitting at the edge of the tee box" in any area of your life? If so, describe the situation.

◄ What is standing in your way?

◄ What is the worst thing that could happen?

◄ What is the best thing that could happen?

◄ What are the Costs/Challenges vs. Benefits (list)

Costs/Challenges vs.   Benefits

_____ /_____

◄ What would be the God-honoring thing to do?

◄ Whatchu waitin' for?

How would you score yourself in the area of *Fear and Mind Games?*

(Scale: Quite well ... Birdie 3; Okay ... Par 4; Needs work ... Bogey 5; A disaster ... Double Bogey 6)

Scorecard

	1	2	3	4	5	6	7	8	9	Out	Total
Par	5	4	4	3	4	4	3	5	4	36	
Yardage	547	409	320	295	363	333	278	454	378	3377	
Score											

	10	11	12	13	14	15	16	17	18	In	
Par	5	4	3	4	4	5	4	4	3	36	
Yardage	498	344	228	329	357	436	340	393	285	3210	6587
Score											

Notes:

Hole #3

Par 4

320 Yards

The Tease of the Tee ...

(Self-Awareness)

A few years ago I had the privilege of playing a new golf course in our area. My excitement had peaked over the previous year as I anxiously waited and watched the course mature to the point it was open for play. This anticipation had been further fueled by conversations I had with a friend of mine who happened to be the designer of the course. In one of our conversations, he shared the vision he had for his latest piece of geographic artwork. As he put it "We tried to give the course a 'rustic look' and used big, sweeping bunkers with fingers of grass drifting into the sand and fescue grasses as lips on the bunker faces."

My first round at the course was a truly memorable experience for me in that it was the first time in more than a decade I had flirted with a sub-80 round. Needless to say, I was enjoying the round immensely, a situation made even more satisfying because I was joined in the round by a good friend with whom I had shared golf for several years. We were scoring decently. My drives were fairly accurate, of good distance and my irons were showing up on the numbers. Life was good! By the time we reached the 14th tee, I was feeling my oats.

Sitting in the cart, waiting for my turn on the tee I checked out the hole description that read:

"This, the shortest of the par 3's, will require precision off the tee. A diverse array of hazards will collect an errant tee shot and may result in an undesirable bogey. Two cavernous bunkers protect the front/left and back/left portions of the green. A deep fairway chipping area falls off the left side of the green, and shots through the green will be collected in a fairway chipping area off the back. The undulating green is the smallest of the par 3's and slopes from right to left. Do not get greedy on this beautiful tree-framed golf hole, and you will set the stage for the finishing holes with par or birdie."

By this time my ego was ballooning. *(Just as an aside, have you ever noticed the inverse relationship between ego and wisdom?)* When it was my turn to play, I checked the actual yardage on the GPS, took note of the fact that it was still somewhat chilly with a temperature somewhere in the low fifties and the wind crossing left to right. All of that taken into account, I stepped to the tee, quickly went through my simple pre-shot routine noting that the flagstick was placed about 15 feet directly behind the leading bunker protecting the left center of the green.

The tease of the pin was irresistible, the two cavernous bunkers notwithstanding. My mind was singing a conqueror's song: *No problem, I'm playing well. I'm going for it. I'll just feather this shot in from the left and allow the wind to move the ball right and back to my target—the flagstick.* With that song filling my head, I pulled the trigger.

I felt the pure rush of adrenalin that accompanies that sense of club and ball connecting in the heart of the sweet spot. I watched as my ball sailed out over the fairway while I held my master-at-work finishing pose.

It rode the wind like an eagle, soaring ever closer to the pin. With exhilaration welling up inside me, I watched as the ball gently descended toward the green, landing just 18 feet short of the pin and directly on track. Unfortunately, it was buried, 3 feet down the slope from the top lip of the front cavernous bunker with its "fingers of fescue grass arching out over its edge."

Aaagh!

In less than five seconds, #14 had morphed from an innocuous little par three to become the eternal bottomless pit, and those beautiful wisps of long fescue grass, lining the bunker my friend had spoken of, had taken on the character of the very fingers of Satan mocking me.

After a short period of self-talk, which does not need to be repeated here, punctuated by absolute silence on the tee, I heard the bright-eyed Mickey Rooney persona in me saying, *Hey, no problem, I'm playing well, just a little adversity, it's all part of the game. I'll just pop that puppy up onto the green, take my lumps, two putt, card my four, and move on, no big deal. Right?*

So went my thinking at least. Unfortunately, my body did not follow the plan so cleverly laid out by Mickey in my head.

Commencing with that touch of mental flagellation over my effort off the tee, shot by shot, my emotions progressed through a sad slideshow:

My second shot—did not exit the bunker as planned ... frustration.

With the third—bunker again ... embarrassment set in.

Stubbornness came visiting on the fourth—the ball, caught by the fescue, returning to the base of the bunker ... my cheeks turning noticeably red.

Confusion and dismay joined the chorus on the fifth—good shot, not high enough, back in the bunker ... where's help when you need it?

Desperation/panic accompanied the sixth—stuck my pick, the ball coming tauntingly to rest two feet away still in the bunker ... more sand in what's left of my hair than is in the bunker.

On the seventh shot, resolve consumed me ... I took a peek and topped it, ... yup, still in the bunker.

And finally, on my eight shot...jubilation! A choir of angels I'm sure could be heard across the golf course, singing, in full voice, the "Hallelujah Chorus" as I escaped the depths of the bunker and landed on the beautiful short grass of the green, finishing the hole in only two additional strokes.

Yes folks, if you are counting, as I was, I carded a 10 on this, the shortest of the par 3s on the course.

As you can accurately surmise, there went the sub-80 round. To make matters worse, my well-meaning playing partner, Tom, in an attempt to triage the situation "wisely" asked me, "Larry, why didn't you just hit the ball sideways out of the bunker into the collect and then knock it on from there, the worst you would probably have taken is a 4 or 5? You had a great round going"—he's a CPA who keeps track of numbers. Really?

(Side note: we don't always appreciate wisdom in the moment it's provided.)
Thank you, Tom!

My sheepish response to Tom is unsettling to me to this day: "I don't know … I never thought of it as an option."

(You might easily be asking *Why not?* We'll come back to that.)

Constructive Reconstruction…

Since that day I have revisited my round and my debacle on #14 many times in my mind. My Navy background and eleven years as a Navigator have schooled me in the practice of debriefing every significant event. We called it "Reconstruction", a process whereby we reviewed the action from beginning to end *as it occurred*—not as we would have liked it to go, but as it actually happened. The purpose has always been to glean every last ounce of learning one can extract from the experience to apply toward future events.

My misadventure at #14 was to me a significant event worthy of "Reconstruction." In looking back, omens of impending disaster started to appear long before we arrived at the 14th tee. Unmerited confidence and pride in how well I was doing showed up as a little swagger in my step and just a moment more reflection time before each putt, intended to send a message to Tom that I was a man confident in his game, playing with purpose.

(Note to self: It's true, pride comes before the fall!)

Voices in my head were saying, *You know, you're really playing over your head, this can't last,* instead of *just focus on this shot—let tomorrow (the next shot) take care of itself.*

(Did you know that's in scripture? Check out Matthew 6:34.)

I was becoming infatuated with, or perhaps even in awe, of my play instead of enjoying the moment—sad but true. When I stepped to the tee I fell for the tease—like a salesman counting his commissions before he makes the sale—*I was focused on the "three" I wanted and now expected to make while paying little attention to what would be necessary to card that three.*

Here are the Facts:

Wind – About a "one-club breeze" coming from left to right – recognized.

Temperature – Chilly – low 50s made cooler by the wind – One more club required – ignored.

Hole Layout – Hole description – *Caution light!* Do not treat this hole casually – trouble front and back with a small side sloping green – ignored.

Architect's Intent – Protect par – How is he doing that? Green slope and bunkers in front - hazards ignored.

Greens Superintendent's Intent – protect par – Sucker pin placement – wisdom ignored.

Club selection – *Caution* (the voice of wisdom) – take one more club than you think you need for easier, more fluid swing, pulled 7 iron, needed the 6 – wisdom ignored.

Target Selection – The pin – "Sucker Pin" appealing to ego and greed and a dishonest read of my core capabilities, ego won - wisdom ignored.

Shot Execution – perfect, well struck, on line ... but one club short – wisdom ignored.

Shots 2 through 7 – Shot selection/execution – Wisdom says the safest way out is to hit to the side of the bunker, take your medicine and chip on from the collect - Wisdom ignored, ego prevailed. Results – 10 strokes.

If this were an aviation accident summary of finding it might read: "Pilot error leading to mechanical malfunction compounded by failure to execute prescribed emergency procedures."

Who cares about my clumsy debacle?

Answer ... I do!

I would prefer to never have another #14 experience for the rest of my days either on the golf course or off. That preference may or may not be honored, but I do have the opportunity to try and stem the tide. I have a choice. I can *choose to learn* from the experience and apply that learning *or roll the dice* hoping that I don't have a similar or worse experience to flog my way through in the future.

I am reminded of a scene from the movie "Bobby Jones: Stroke of Genius." In this particular scene involving Jones and sportswriter O. B. Keller discussing a match that Jones has just lost, Bobby says to O.B., "I never learned anything from a tournament I won."

In essence, he was saying: "It's the losses, the challenging experiences, that are my teachers." O.B., in response to Bobby, reminds him of a Will Rogers comment: "Good judgment comes from experience, and a lot of that experience comes from bad judgment."

Both Jones and Keller's comments are instructional and encouraging to me. I have come to look forward to the process of constructive reconstruction, not as a process of self-inflicted flogging intended to highlight my ineptness, but as a process of identifying what I need to do differently in the future so that I can improve my game, apply better judgment and enjoy it more.

I am buoyed by the fact that I can choose to learn and grow 'til the day I die.

The Good News...

First – Hole #14 was a difficult experience for me, fraught with bad judgment. But there is good news to share as well. From what I have learned through this experience I can—if I pay attention to my lessons learned—readily cut at least five strokes off my score, on that hole, simply by listening to the voice of wisdom as opposed to overriding it, not to mention what might happen if I ever get my sand game under control.

(To the latter, I like Harvey Penick's approach to the bunker challenge: "Let's learn not to go there.")

Second – Having chosen to keep trying and remain in the game as opposed to picking up/giving up and disengaging, I have a sense of accomplishment and victory—I persevered. It is my prayer to persevere in *every aspect of my life* until I finally hear that choir of angels sing for real ... in person on into eternity.

Why didn't you...?

Back to the pesky question, "Why didn't you just hit the ball sideways into the collect?" The honest answer is ego! However, I think, a less painful, more constructive question to ask is "What did I learn?"

What did I learn? Four primary things:

- Be aware of what the future might hold but focus on today and the moment within the day. Dedicate yourself to the moment. How are you doing in this area? Do you have anything coming up that's got you worried?

- Stop trying to impress others, let your behavior speak for itself. Honesty check: How's the ego doing?

- Consider the wisdom of others—don't merely hear it! Are you open to good counsel, or are you more of a giver in that area?

- Consider the cost before taking the shot. Ask, "What is advisable?" This is an area in which one can easily stumble. How often do you fail to consider the cost before you take action?

Work for the Practice Range:

◄ Have you ever had a #14 experience—on or off the golf course? (Part of the learning process is sharing. Describe it.)

◄ Have you insisted on reconstructing those experiences to learn all you can from them? Did you write down what you have learned?

◄ If so, what have you learned?

◄ From where or from whom have you sought help? Remember, like it or not, life is a team sport.

How would you score yourself in the area of ***Self-Awareness?***

(Scale: Quite well ... Birdie 3; Okay ... Par 4; Needs work ... Bogey 5; A disaster ... Double Bogey 6)

Scorecard

	1	2	3	4	5	6	7	8	9	Out	Total
Par	5	4	4	3	4	4	3	5	4	36	
Yardage	547	409	320	295	363	333	278	454	378	3377	
Score											

	10	11	12	13	14	15	16	17	18	In	
Par	5	4	3	4	4	5	4	4	3	36	
Yardage	498	344	228	329	357	436	340	393	285	3210	6587
Score											

Notes:

Hole #4

Par 3

295 Yards

To Trust, or Not to Trust?

(Trust)

"Trust: **a belief in,** *assured reliance on the character, ability, strength, integrity, or truth of someone or something, confident expectation."*

– *Merriam Webster*

Larry Joliffe...

Go ahead and ask. "Who in the world is Larry Joliffe and why are you bringing up his name?"

During the tenure of my very first job in the corporate sector (circa 1965–1967), Larry was a work colleague of mine. We both worked in the sales department of, the now defunct, Clark Equipment Company. He was a product sales manager and I was a sales trainee in the same office, although not under his tutelage.

Larry was probably 15 years my senior. He was an avid golfer in his spare time and would often regale us with his latest weekend golfing exploits. At that juncture in my life, I was a fledgling golfer, relishing playing with anyone who would tolerate a novice.

The vision of my first and only time I ever joined Larry for a round of golf resides permanently in my memory. We played on the original course of what is now a six-course complex known as the Gull Lake View Golf Club and Resort, which today enjoys marquee status in southern Michigan. In 1965, however, it looked to me like the grazing land for dairy cows with occasional flagsticks scattered here and there across the gently rolling landscape.

Why do I remember these details so vividly? Because, it was on the third par 3 of that course, that I learned a very important and lasting lesson from the links. It's a lesson that has served me well for now over fifty years.

Larry had invited me and two other guys for a Saturday round of golf on, as he described it, "this new course just a few miles from here." At the time I had never played with Larry, so I knew very little about his golf game, his character, or his demeanor on the golf course. I simply considered it an honor that he would include me in his invitation to play.

Lesson day...

The day was overcast with westerly fall breezes in the air. Throughout the first few holes, it became obvious that Larry had more than just a modicum of golf skill. He carded lower scores on a considerable majority of the holes we played, earning him first off the tee honors frequently throughout our round. Thus was the case as we approached our first of two par 3s on the backside of the course. Larry had "honors"—the privilege of teeing off first.

He took a moment to check the breeze, the yardage to the green and selected a club from his bag. After ceremoniously sticking his tee in the ground and meticulously placing his ball on it, he took a couple practice swings. Basking in the spotlight of our undivided attention—his body language inviting us to watch the master—he slowly stepped into address position over his ball. After pausing momentarily to allow his fan base of three to quiet, he triggered his swing, sending the ball flying, as if it had eyes, straight toward the pin. When the ball came to rest he had only a short "gimme" putt left for a birdie two.

Being a 20-year-old kid with less than a year's worth of golf experience to my name, I was duly impressed with his effort. After the obligatory "nice shot" compliments from those of us on the tee, and waiting for my other two playing partners to hit, it was my turn.

Not knowing it was considered "poor form" to ask such a question, I turned to Larry and innocently asked, "What iron did you hit there?"

He looked at me with a big tooth-filled grin on his face and said, "A 7 iron."

With that information in hand, I pulled a 7 iron from my bag and stepped to the tee. I hit the ball fairly well and it too headed toward the green. To my amazement—and Larry's amusement—the ball sailed over the pin and went on to settle in knee-high weeds a full twenty yards beyond the green.

Once Larry got his uproarious laughter under control he turned to me and asked, "What did you hit?"

I answered, somewhat quizzically, "A 7 iron."

Still unable to contain his amusement he blurted, "Really? Are you that stupid? I hit a 9 iron."

At that point, I was too dumbfounded to offer any responsible rejoinder.

(Read, there were a number of things I was tempted to say, including some about his parentage, but did not.)

Today, reliving the moment, I can still resurrect the feelings of gullibility and embarrassment that engulfed me as I stood there on the tee, the object of my playing partners' amusement. "Are you really that stupid?"

The lesson—painfully seared to my mental hide long before President Ronald Reagan coined the phrase—"Trust … but verify!"

Fast-forward five years and the gravity of that early lesson from the links (i.e., the story of Mr. Joliffe's undeserved trust) took on a more global and serious note. By that time, I was a Lieutenant in the U.S. Navy, a designated Naval Flight Officer (NFO), and Flight Crew Mission Commander. In that capacity, I was responsible for my combat readiness as well as that of the six men in my tactical flight crew.

During our final readiness check, prior to a six-month deployment to Vietnam, my flight crew—along with all eleven other flight crews in our squadron—was required to demonstrate a portion of our readiness by participating in a weapons/ordnance loading inspection, both for safety and tactical reasons.

As a part of that inspection, we were tasked with loading out our aircraft with combat ordnance (bombs, rockets, torpedos and wing-mounted cannons) as if we were preparing to carry out a mission. This was considered serious business. It was so serious that, if we failed inspection, our squadron would not be allowed to deploy and our Commanding Officer's job would be in jeopardy.

The loading process was filled with a myriad of safety precautions and procedures, each with its own distinct checklist. My job was to ensure that everything was done safely and by the book. According to "the book," as a safety precaution during the loading inspection, all ordnance "off/drop toggle switches" were to be "hard-wired" in the off position.

At the completion of our loading sequence, my loading chief reported to me, as was required, that all weapons were loaded and ready for inspection.

I responded, "Very well."

That's Navy lingo for "I have heard and understand."

As a final precaution, with the lesson "trust ... but verify" blinking like a yellow caution light in my memory, I decided to take one final walk through and around the aircraft to verify that everything was, in fact, ready for inspection. To my dismay, I found one of the weapon's "off/drop toggle switches" erroneously hard-wired in the drop position—a major blunder!

Fortunately, we were able to stop the load and correct the error prior to our final inspection review. Had I not taken the time to verify the information I had been given by my loading chief, the damages from an accidentally jettisoned weapon could have been catastrophic.

As a result of episodes such as those just mentioned—which occurred fairly early in my adult life—I have had a keen interest in what else the game of golf and the golf course might have to teach me about trust in my life. Now, some fifty years into my observations on the subject, I am still learning.

I am amazed at how often trust shows up as a player on the golf course. If you haven't thought about it before, take a moment and walk with me through just a few instances where I see a need for trust in my game:

- If I am honestly in pursuit of a better golf game, I must start before I even get to the golf course by getting enough rest so that I can trust my body to perform, as I desire.

- I have to trust that I have practiced to proficiency my swing mechanics so that my body will deliver a good swing ... on demand.

- I must trust that I can honestly assess my strengths and weaknesses, not letting my ego sway my assessment of each situation I face on the golf course and make appropriate adjustments where necessary—whether mid-round or between, on my own, or, with the help of a trusted coach.

- I have to trust my "feel," to effectively execute my pitching, chipping, and putting.

- Regarding my body, I must trust and appropriately respond to its signals that tell me when I need fluids, nutrition, or a pause to rest.

- Trusting my analytical capabilities is an essential component in deciding how, and with what club, I approach each shot. I must pay attention to and trust the available data and my memory bank in making each decision.

- Once on the course, I must trust in the equipment I have, to play the game I want to play. I must also trust that I have the right amount of equipment in my bag to stay within the rules of the game—more than 14 clubs in the bag and a penalty is assessed.

- If I am fortunate enough to have the services of a caddie, I have a choice to make. Do I see my caddie as merely a pack mule, or do I trust them to not only carry my bag but give me sound on-course advice as well?

Over the years I have come to believe that trust is a perilously fragile commodity. It can take years to build and seconds to destroy, whether it's on the golf course or other facets of my life. My desire is to value and continue to build on those trust relationships I enjoy today. For me to do so takes continued attention to detail, keeping a constant weather eye out for the storms of life that can put a damper on that trust.

I have learned to revere the position that trust holds in playing good golf and the every day living out of a good life. Over time I have observed that trust is a product of my expectations, *which must be followed by verification.* It is also important to note, not all expectations merit my trust. Some of those expectations are rooted in fantasy. My responsibility is to assiduously root out the fantasy and tenaciously hang on to what I know to be real and true.

A final thought...

I would be remiss if I didn't share this last thought about trust, made so clear to me through the years of my golfing experience. You have, I'm sure, heard from time to time the phrase in golf, "You have to trust your swing."

I have found I need to trust my life swing as well. As a result, I have a checklist housed in my heart that I am challenged to visit frequently. It includes the following:

- What ongoing behaviors do I exhibit that indicate or verify I can be trusted?

- Who can I trust to go to for help?

- How do I know I can trust the helper?

I do not possess all the answers I want to these questions. I do know, however, whom I can trust implicitly in every situation. The reason I know I can trust Him is that He loved me so much that He (my Maker) sent His Son to rescue me ... from me.

He expunged all of my misadventures (sin), asking nothing in return but that I trust and accept His Gift, and follow his lead. For that, I am eternally grateful. I did not deserve his gift of rescue, but he provided it anyway. That's verification enough for me to unequivocally trust Him.

How about you? Where, and in who, are you putting your implicit trust, and how do you know you can trust them?

Work for the Practice Range:

◄ Have you ever acted on information you were given by someone you trusted only to find out later the information you were given was not true? Y/N

◄ What were your feelings about yourself when you found out the truth? (Describe)

◄ What were your feelings about the individual or individuals who provided you with the untruth? (Describe)

◄ Have you ever provided information to someone else, only to find out later it was not true? Y/N

◄ If your answer to the previous question was "Yes," how did you deal with the situation? (Describe)

◄ How can you verify your truths before you pass them on? (Describe)

How would you score yourself in the area of ***Trust?***
(Scale: Quite well ... Birdie 2; Okay ... Par 3; Needs work ...
Bogey 4; A disaster ... Double Bogey 5)

Scorecard

	1	2	3	4	5	6	7	8	9	Out	Total
Par	5	4	4	3	4	4	3	5	4	36	
Yardage	547	409	320	295	363	333	278	454	378	3377	
Score											

	10	11	12	13	14	15	16	17	18	In	
Par	5	4	3	4	4	5	4	4	3	36	
Yardage	498	344	228	329	357	436	340	393	285	3210	6587
Score											

Notes:

Hole #5

Par 4

363 Yards

Margin ... Who Needs Margin?

(Margin)

Are you anything like me? Are you one of those people who makes a habit—consciously or not—of cutting things close, i.e., getting things done or arriving at places just in the nick of time? If so, you might enjoy revisiting the "Keystone Cops"–style vignette that played out during the early stages of the 2012 Ryder Cup matches between the U.S. and Europe.

The main character in this little piece of golf drama is European player, Rory McIlroy.

Story has it that young McIlroy had momentarily lost sight of the fact that he was playing in a different time zone than that of his homeland, Ireland. He was still in his hotel room when—like a shot of electricity through his system—the error in his thinking hit home. At that moment, still miles away from the starting tee at Medinah Country Club, he was confronted with the reality that failure to appear in a timely fashion for his scheduled tee time would result in immediate disqualification from the Ryder Cup competition.

What ensued was a mad dash from his hotel—complete with police escort service, sirens howling—to the portico of the Medinah clubhouse. This was followed by a frenzied sprint—like someone who should have answered nature's call an hour earlier—across the bridge between the clubhouse and the first tee, arriving with just enough time to check in with the tournament starter and tee off.

While he did narrowly miss immediate disqualification without ever firing a shot, he did not avoid the ire of some of his teammates and the displeasure of golfing enthusiasts across the continent of Europe, as exemplified in the tongue-in-cheek comment of one European journalist who wrote, "On such an important day as this, you would imagine the players might arrive early. Not Rory McIlroy—he almost missed his tee off time." – Mike Blake/Reuters

All of this drama was telecast across the U.S. and Europe ... LIVE!

The "McIlroy scramble" still plays vividly in my memory as if I were sitting, back in our den, face glued to the TV, watching the saga unfold and somewhat judgmentally thinking, *Man I'll bet he would have appreciated a little margin for warm-up and practice. What was he thinking?*

(Before moving on, it is important that we give Mr. McIlroy a bit of grace here. Having traveled the country relentlessly, during portions of my career, I can thoroughly empathize with how a person can momentarily lose track of what city, much less which time zone, they are in. I would also be remiss if I didn't recognize that he went on to win his match that day.)

Today, with Rory's misadventure, already several years in the rear view mirror, I am tempted to be a little smug in my thinking—*Better you than me pal. I would never let that happen to me.*

With that thought still fresh in my mind, however, I feel a not-so-gentle nudge from on high saying, "Really? Is that true?" And, just that fast, I am confronted, from within, with a challenge ...

"Hey, Mr. 'Holier Than Thou', aren't you the same guy who frequently would dash down an airport concourse, trip up the escalator and arrive in the boarding area of your intended flight, clothes in disarray, sweating like a dog, just in time to be the last passenger crossing the threshold of the cabin as the flight attendant was reaching for the handle to close the aircraft door directly behind you? And ... do you remember the flights you missed by following that same well-worn practice?"

These episodes of self-centered frenzy, which impacted not only me but those around me as well, were due to my misplaced priorities and a selfish attitude, i.e., I treated my agenda as more important than yours, "better you wait for me than I wait for you."

The obvious truth is, I did not take the time or make the effort, to put in my schedule the modicum of margin necessary to allow things to run more smoothly.

The incidents referenced above are but a few of the examples of poor planning, less than stellar thinking and insufficient installation of margin on my part. I have a whole litany of examples to choose from, many of which are episodes that have occurred within my family that are too personally painful and would serve no constructive purpose to resurrect here.

I share this personal sample here only to help open the door to your own library of margin reminiscence. If you are at all like me, your library of margin missteps runs the gamut from insignificant moments to situations with painful consequences.

Hmmm...

My purpose in bringing the subject of margin to the fore is simply to suggest that there is something we might all be reminded of from Mr. McIlroy's incident. (Remember my premise that golf is a marvelous metaphor for life?)

His example, broadcast worldwide, dramatically illustrates a challenge I— and perhaps you—face daily, which is bigger than golf alone. I am challenged to look at the ripple effects that can occur when margin is not given its due.

As a point of clarification, when I use the term "margin", I intend it to mean... *that spare amount or measure of time, space or degree allowed to accommodate a given situation.*

We who golf are inextricably dependent on the wise application of margin as we play. We call it "taking into account "or "making allowance" for such things as the wind, playing altitude, temperature, weather, contour of the green, our physical condition, type of grass we are playing on, depth of the rough, location of any hazards, consistency of the sand in the hazard, pin placement, out of bounds markers, our club selection, our skills and more.

As I ponder the whole issue of margin, I am surprised at how many times per day I am confronted with decisions regarding the right amount of margin for a given situation. From the moment I rise in the morning to the point at which I rest at night, and even as I drift into sleep, the issue of appropriate margin is a constant companion.

In fact, the last thing I check before crawling into bed at night is whether my alarm is set to wake me in time to prepare for and meet the challenges of the day ahead (i.e., have I planned enough margin into my schedule?).

From Golf to God, and everything in between, I have much room for growth and additional wisdom in my planning. I am not, as yet, a consummate "marginista." I am, however, striving to establish better margins as the guardrails through which to traverse my life.

Below, I have listed a few areas of margin challenges in my life, broken down by category, that I feel might be enriched, should I choose to be more attentive to them. As you will readily note, my lists are not all-inclusive, nor am I suggesting that any of the items on my lists should be on yours. My sole motivation for sharing my lists with you—the reader—is the hope that you, a fellow traveler in this life, might be inclined to do a little "margin needs identification and installation" of your own. As such, please feel free to use my example as a starter template.

Margin in my Family Life:

- Am I <u>self</u>-focused or <u>others</u>-focused? (My family is not nearly as interested in the margins I adhere to as I make my way around a golf course as they are about the margins I adhere to as I approach life within our family unit.)

- Do I have the capacity for, and a desire, to extend love, space, and grace—all of which are types of margin—to those in need?

- Do I have the wisdom to request a little margin (to take some time to breathe) as we work our way through some of our issues?

(Issues such as family values, respect for one another, time, time thieves, valuation of media input or encroachment, use of digital technology, age, geography, and more, all need attention and some kind of margin quotient in my family life.)

Margin in my Social Life:

While I don't necessarily like it, I am confronted with establishing a myriad of social margin criteria. The amount of time, energy, heart, and soul I choose to allocate in my social interactions differs dramatically depending upon the relationship or circumstance. I have become much more selective as to what, or with whom, I am willing to give bits and pieces of my most valuable commodity—my time.

Margin comes in many forms as one looks at the mental, physical, and emotional aspects of the social arena:

- Personal Space – Whom do I let inside and whom do I keep at a distance?

- Trust – Whom do I trust? How much should I trust? How close do I let others get to me?

- Respect – Whom do I respect? How much respect do I proffer each individual? (For me it varies—Love is a requirement, respect is earned.)

- Love – Is my commitment to love conditional or unconditional?

- Grace – Am I willing to extend some space, slack or unmerited forgiveness—margin—to those I choose to embrace in my social environment?

- Regarding Commitments – Do my actions reflect my stated commitments or is there a bit of space—negative margin—between what I commit to and what actually transpires?

- Physical Geography – How am I handling my long-distance relationships? How much energy am I putting into those relationships?

- Emotional Geography – How do I define the difference between acquaintance, friend, and inner circle?

Margin in my Intellectual Life:

- Do I fill my mind with intellectual junk food or do I make room (create margin) to dine on fine intellectual cuisine?

- Do I make time to feed my intellectual appetite regularly or do I tend to just snack in that area?

- Do I seek out and harbor any intellectually or spiritually destructive mind feeds or do I mindfully avoid those contributors, as I would a lake or a bunker on the golf course?

Margin in my Career Life:

- What efforts do I put forth to stay enthusiastic about and enjoy my work? What margins, both physically and emotionally, are required?

- Am I getting enough rest/downtime to allow me to do my best job?

- Am I working in the mainstream of my passion? If not at present, am I willing to carve out time—margin—in my schedule to move in the direction of my passion?

- Am I employing the full range of skills, gifts, and talents I possess? This is an area where I cannot afford margin. (The question is, am I giving the best of myself, or am holding back a bit?)

Margin in my Financial Life:

- Do I meet my financial obligations with margin to spare at the end of each month?

- Do I carry large credit balances (more than I can pay off in six months)?

- Do I make a habit of saving at least 10% of my take-home income?

- Do I invest only in things I understand?

- Do I put God first in the management of my financial assets?

- Am I generous with resources I have access to or do I believe my budget is too tight for me to be generous?

- Am I living basically debt free (sans mortgage)?

(Confession: Financial Margin is an area in which I have historically struggled – LG)

Margin in my Physical Life:

- Do I have healthy eating habits?

- Do I have appropriate healthy relationships with alcohol, drug, and tobacco products?

- Do I exercise daily in a healthy fashion?

- Do I get rest and sleep appropriate for my age and level of activity?

- Do I get the appropriate medical checkups and inspections recommended by my doctor?

- Do I pay attention to the ailment signals my body provides and seek medical counsel, when necessary? Or do I wait until my health reaches an emergency level?

- Do I monitor and moderate the stress levels in my life?

- Do I include recreation as an adjunct to my exercise regimen?

Margin in my Spiritual Life:

- Am I experiencing a spiritual void in my life at present?

- Am I knowledgeable regarding the foundations of my beliefs, i.e., do I know why I believe what I believe, or is this an area of slush?

- Am I mindful of my beliefs and strive to live them out on a daily basis?

- Is my spiritual life the hub around which my daily life rotates, or do I treat it as one of several peripheral aspects of my life?

- Am I at peace (settled/comfortable) with my beliefs—i.e., ready to bet my life on them?

Why am I making such a big deal about margin?

Why? Because, in so doing, I play better, enjoy the game more, experience greater satisfaction and joy, and earn more respect, and self-respect—especially when things go well. Why wouldn't I do everything I can, including the adherence to appropriate margins, to play my best?

Golf—as much as I love the game and all it provides—is just a game. Yet, I spend substantial amounts of mental and physical energy, time, and resources, attempting to play the best I can. Doesn't it make sense for me to apply similar amounts of mental and physical energy, time, appropriate resources, and margin in the other facets of my life outside of golf to play the best I can in those arenas as well?

Like it or not we all are faced with that same dilemma today. As my commanding officer, Captain Freund, used to say, *"We've got all the time they is, they ain't makin' any more."*

In today's world, the beggars of our time seem to be constantly increasing. The reality is we must establish margin in our lives, whether we want to or not. To fail to do so is to invite mental saturation, high stress, depleted joy, and potential physical and spiritual harm.

It is a lie that we have to be all things to all people. That is not true. What is true is that we are one hundred percent responsible for how we choose to spend our time and keep our sanity.

To you, the reader and hopefully fellow golfer, I have one final and very personal thought to share:

If you have not yet made your decision and put your plan in place as to where you intend to spend your (eternal) future—you still have the remainder of your life as margin. But remember, margin is a wasted asset if you don't employ it. What you don't take advantage of, you lose. Each indecisive day you allow is one less day of margin available to you. So there is urgency for you to do your homework and from your homework make reasoned—notice I said reasoned, not impulsive—decisions regarding the self-imposed margins you initiate, while you still have time remaining on the clock of your life.

(See John 3:16, Romans 3:21–28 and 10:9–10, *Holy Bible*)

Work for the Practice Range:

Is there any planning—including the installation of appropriate margins—you need to put in place:

◄ In your Family life? Yes/No   If so what might they be?

◄ In your Social Life? Yes/No   If so what might they be?

◄ In your Intellectual Life? Yes/No   If so what might they be?

◄ In your Career? Yes/No   If so what might they be?

◄ In your Financial Life? Yes/No   If so what might they be?

◄ In your Physical Life? Yes/No   If so what might they be?

◄ In your Spiritual Life? Yes/No   If so what might they be?

How would you score yourself in the area of **Margin,** and would your family agree with your assessment?

(Scale: Quite well ... Birdie 3; Okay ... Par 4; Needs work ... Bogey 5; A disaster ... Double Bogey 6)

Scorecard

	1	2	3	4	5	6	7	8	9	Out	Total
Par	5	4	4	3	4	4	3	5	4	36	
Yardage	547	409	320	295	363	333	278	454	378	3377	
Score											

	10	11	12	13	14	15	16	17	18	In	
Par	5	4	3	4	4	5	4	4	3	36	
Yardage	498	344	229	329	357	436	340	393	285	3210	6587
Score											

Notes:

Hole #6

Par 4

333 Yards

A Vision, a Swamp, and a Buck

(Vision)

Stephen Covey, in his book *Seven Habits of Highly Effective People*, postulated: "effective" (i.e., successful) people "begin with the end in mind." In short, they have a vision.

My friends at Merriam-Webster say vision is "The act or power of seeing i.e., sight with all of its biological processes, a thought or concept formed in the mind but not yet manifest in reality, an act or power of imagination, and a phenomenon of unusual discernment or foresight."

A "Must See" Tournament ...

Keeping in mind the all-inclusive definition of vision—as stated above—a great representation of that vision would be the famous TPC Sawgrass Stadium Golf Course in Ponte Vedra, Florida. One of my must see tournaments in the spring of each year is played at TPC Sawgrass, on the "Stadium Course." We, who track such things, consider the Sawgrass tournament to be the "unofficial fifth Major of the year."

This unique golf course is a considerable drawing card for the Sawgrass Marriott Golf Resort and Spa. The Players Championship has been hosted by the Sawgrass facility since 1982 for several reasons. Chief among those reasons is that the PGA Tour Professionals own the golf course.

This happy circumstance of ownership by the tour professionals did not come to fruition by accident. It was the brainchild (vision) of a very thoughtful and creative man by the name of Deane Beman.

According to the TPC.com website, "In the mid-1970s, shortly after Beman commenced his reign as the second PGA Commissioner, he shared a vision, with those who would listen, to create a unique host site for The Players Championship."

(It is important to note that the Players Championship was, at that time, the only tournament owned by the members of the PGA Tour.)

It didn't just happen. Beman had a vision. His goal was to:

- Create a permanent home of The Players Championship, that would be owned by the PGA tour members.

- Build the first true "Stadium Course," designed and built to improve the overall on-site fan experience.

- Create TPC Sawgrass to be a course of great design and character, as much for the spectators as for the players.

(Note: At the time of construction nearly all of the great tournaments were played at private clubs where the average fan rarely had a chance to play.)

Beman first approached the owners of Sawgrass Country Club, the Arvida Corporation, and offered to buy their facility. Not only did they not want to sell, they didn't believe the commissioner would ever get financing or approval to buy a facility. Arvida Chairman Charles Cobb even proposed a $100 business sportsmanship bet—his words, not mine—with Beman that he could never achieve his vision.

Undeterred, Beman sought other options to stay in the Ponte Vedra Beach area, eventually finding allies in Jerome and Paul Fletcher, two of the major landowners in the area. They believed in Beman's dream so much that they sold/ donated 415 acres of wooded wetlands and swamp to the PGA Tour—complete with gators and snakes—for $1.00.

And so with vision/purpose, passion, and land in hand, the plan began to take shape. Calling on the architectural genius of Alice and Pete Dye, Beman specified that he wanted a course design that would favor no particular player or style of play.

To meet this goal, an extensive effort was made to design a balanced golf course. There had to be:

- A selection of short, medium, and long holes (par 3s, par 4s, and par 5s).

- Both right and left doglegs.

- Routed in such a fashion that no two consecutive holes played in the same direction, thus requiring the golfer to pay continual attention to the ever-changing winds.

This set of parameters led to a need to move massive amounts of soil from one location to another. For the first time, spectator viewing was given full consideration in the design and layout of a golf course. The construction site, a north Florida wetland—a kind descriptor for a swamp—was flat and heavily wooded.

The Dyes noted that there were no areas on the construction site with an elevation greater than 18 inches above the waterline. As a result of that insight, lakes were created not only for strategic, thoughtful play but also to provide a much-needed source of fill material to create the contours of the playing area and stadium mounding.

An unexpected by-product of the lake construction was the birthing of the 137-yard, par 3, 17th hole. The original design of the hole called for a small pond near the intended green. However, during the excavation for the site, a large deposit of useable sand was discovered and mined for use on other parts of the course. The result of that mining left a cavernous hole, consuming most of the area around what was to be the green, which ended up being both a challenge and a serendipitous windfall for the architects.

When Alice Dye, Pete's wife, saw the dramatic effects of the sand harvesting around the intended green, she called on the designers' flexibility and creativity suggesting that they take advantage of the situation and change the design of the hole to that of an island green.

It is now, unquestionably, one of the most famous and revered par-3s in the world.

When the club was finally built and about to officially open, Beman received a special plaque marking the occasion in March 1980. It showcased a $100 bill, which is on display in the clubhouse, with this inscription:

> "To Deane Beman, the man who did what we said couldn't be done. From Chuck Cobb and his associates at Arvida, *who bet on the difficulty of the task, not on the capability of the man doing the task.*"
> ** (Emphasis mine – LG)*

TPC Sawgrass is only one of a significant list of broad-based initiatives Beman put into play, including skippering the growth of PGA tour assets during his tenure, from $400,000 in 1974 to a reported $260 million twenty years later.

The driving power of vision/purpose, fueled by passion, never ceases to amaze me. Beman's vision has produced fruit far beyond his expectations and multiple Stadium Courses now exist because of his vision.

Why is this story a highlight in my mind? Why might you or I care?

My answer comes from the realm of personal experience. Throughout my life, my primary forms of learning have been, 1) The school of hard knocks and 2) My observation of other successful people.

I tend to try to emulate—or take my inspiration from—the behaviors of others, whom I respect, and in whom I have seen success. *(That is why I have throughout my adult life always had a Sea Daddy or two—read mentors—in my life from whom I draw direction and in whom I can confide.)*

While I have never met Mr. Beman, I can still learn from him as I look at some of the key factors that made his tenure at the helm of the PGA so successful.

His success with TPC Sawgrass is indeed impressive. Not, however, unexpected, given the steps he took as leader of the project. He followed through with some tried and true concepts. He knew that one casts a vision with words; making their vision a reality, however, takes action, dedication, creativity, flexibility, and tremendous perseverance. And he proved up to the task.

Among other things, he:

- Had a vision in his mind's eye.

- Owned the vision to which he committed mind, body, and soul.

- Was convinced that it was the right thing to do.

- Invested his blood, sweat, and tears, transforming his vision into an action plan.

- Exhibited the courage, dedication, and perseverance necessary to stay the course and execute the plan, in spite of the naysayers who were literally betting he would fail.

I can learn from Mr. Beman's example. Science has undisputedly determined, via DNA, we are each uniquely designed, in the womb, no two alike, with the seeds of our future giftedness and interests in place to spring forth and mature over time.

(Which means I most likely will not be developing "the next TPC Sawgrass." – L.G.)

I can, however, pursue my vision with passion and energy, just as Mr. Beman has done, knowing that our Maker has invested in me the gifts and the skills to follow my own vision, even though I too am not financially equipped to do so at the moment. One step at a time, one challenge at a time I can continue in my quest to pursue my vision.

I do not believe that the message I have derived from Mr. Beman's example is meant solely for me, nor is it a new message.

The first four chapters of the New Testament of my Bible chronicle the events of the world's greatest visionary to ever walk this planet. Over two thousand years ago Jesus came and spent a significant amount of his thirty-three years with us, casting a vision of what life would eventually be like for those who choose to follow him.

During that period of time He

- Shared the vision of things to come.

- Owned the vision to which he committed mind, body, soul, and life.

- Was convinced that it was the right thing to do.

- Invested his blood, sweat, and tears, transforming his vision into an action plan.

- Exhibited the courage, dedication, and perseverance necessary to stay the course and execute the plan, in spite of the naysayers who were literally betting he would fail.

Some believed him, many scoffed him and others even gambled on his not being successful in what he projected in his vision. Yet three days after being put to death, supposedly for the heresy of that proclaimed vision, He rose again, just as He had foretold. In essence, those who bet against him bet on the difficulty of the task, not on the capability of the man doing the task.

He did exactly what he said he would do. He rose from the dead, walked around, and ate among those same people and forty days later ascended into the clouds while over five hundred witnesses watched as he ascended after casting one last vision: "I will return."

What a vision! And what a day that will be!

One rather sobering question I take away from the two examples provided above is:

What will I do with the vision I've been given?

The choice is mine...

Deane Beman had neither the skills nor the assets to build TPC Sawgrass, yet he did. He did so by putting his skills and determination to the task and enlisting the help of others, once again proving to me that life is not a solo race. I will always need the inclusion of others to bring my vision to fruition.

Sadly, for a variety of reasons, I sometimes choose to demur and pass the baton of my life on to others and live under the stifling presumption that "I am not capable, or, my vision is too big, so why try?" The unfortunate, yet predictable result of such a presumption is that it leads to disappointment, loss of self-respect, frustration, and an ever chiding comment in the soul that says, *"I coulda, but I didn't."*

I project, through my faith in the words of Jesus, that someday in the future I will stand, alone, before my Maker and be asked the straightforward question: "I gave you a set of gifts and talents and the opportunity to employ them. What happened? What did you do with those gifts and the plans I had for you to use them?

I am confident that the response, "I did not try because I didn't think I could do it," would raise a serious eyebrow from the throne.

If you are having difficulty making any sense or deriving any purpose currently in your life, please take note, as I have, from a friend of mine, golf course architect, Rick Jacobson who shared this with me:

"If you want to know what the golf course architect had in mind for each hole of their design, go to the green and look back to the tee and you will see the purpose of the plan."

I believe a strong life corollary to Rick's comment might be this:

If you want to know what the Creator (God) had in mind when He blessed your parents with the privilege of bringing you into this world, from the green of your life—your current position—look back over the course of your life. As you do, identify the high spots, i.e., those areas where you derived the greatest sense of fulfillment, the situations in which you excelled, and those in which you experienced genuine long lasting joy. The trail you see is a glimpse of the Designer's purpose in your creation and a reservoir to draw from, moving forward.

One final note...

I find much more satisfaction, fulfillment and joy in my life when I am applying my gifts and talents in pursuit of a vision larger than myself. It's a conscious choice each of us gets to make—self or greater than self.

Crafting a great, invigorating golf course is a beautiful thing. Crafting a great, productive, invigorating life is even more beautiful. We have a part to play in both arenas.

The reality is, once finished with our games—both golf and life—we then have the privilege of having our games reviewed and our scores posted. *Our golf score will be recalled, perhaps throughout history. Our life score will last eternally.*

Work for the Practice Range:

◄ Looking back from the present over the resume of your life, what high points do you see in your history? Where have you excelled? What have you enjoyed most?

◄ Give yourself a moment to reflect on your pursuits in life. Where have you been the strongest? Where have you given back?

◄ What brings you greater joy ... giving or getting? Explain why.

◄ In what areas of your life do you perceive improvement might be helpful?

◄ What do you perceive your purpose or vision in life to be?

◄ What are you doing with the gifts God gave you?

◄ What will you do with what you have discovered about yourself?

How would you score yourself in the area of ***Vision?***

(Scale: Quite well ... Birdie 3; Okay ... Par 4; Needs work ... Bogey 5; A disaster ... Double Bogey 6)

Scorecard

	1	2	3	4	5	6	7	8	9	Out	Total
Par	5	4	4	3	4	4	3	5	4	36	
Yardage	547	409	320	295	363	333	278	454	378	3377	
Score											

	10	11	12	13	14	15	16	17	18	In	
Par	5	4	3	4	4	5	4	4	3	36	
Yardage	498	344	228	329	357	436	340	393	285	3210	6587
Score											

Notes:

Hole #7

Par 3

278 Yards

Hazards ...

(Focus)

"Wow...there's a lot of trouble out there..."

Above are the words uttered by my then-teenage daughter, Layne, over thirty years ago, as we stepped to the tee of the #1 handicap hole of one of my favorite courses in our area. I wish I had been prescient enough to share my all-time favorite Golf instructor Harvey Penick's words—"take dead aim"—with her at the time, but they were not yet in print.

What Layne was concerned about, in her observation, was the seeming preponderance of hazards she needed to be aware of and avoid when playing the hole. I couldn't help thinking then, as I do now, *Welcome to life sweetie, welcome to life!* I can remember musing, *What better place to begin to pay attention to those things that lie ahead that can hinder, distract, or even deny your opportunity to reach the target or destination of your choosing.*

To be clear, on the golf course, a hazard is an obstacle, either natural or man-made, which could contribute to an unfavorable result should you happen to cross the line and enter its territory. Examples are bunkers, ponds, lakes, creeks, etc., and out-of-bounds markers, which line the perimeter of the playing area. Also to be considered here, although not referenced as hazards, are the messages starting with "I should" or "I shouldn't" as well as the fuzzy "what if" questions that dance in my head and distract my thinking.

In the early days of golf—circa A.D. 1500–1600—the game was played on the rough grassy areas between the sea and the land, on the eastern coast of Scotland, hence the name "Links." During that era, the entire playing surface would have looked like one giant hazard.

In time, as more people began to play the game, golf course development moved inland from the coast. Course designers of ongoing generations, in keeping with the original spirit of the old courses, incorporated bunkers (sand traps) and water hazards as baseline components in their design.

I have found golf to be a beautiful and challenging opportunity to face the hazards of the golf course and sharpen my capacity to persevere, not necessarily to chase perfection—although that is laudable—but to reinforce that voice in me that says, "You can do this" in other facets of my life as well.

I also take great pleasure in silencing the beast within (the negative voice) that says, "You should just give up. You're no good at this." It is, in part, the energy I derive from winning the battle with the beast that brings me back to the game again and again.

In his writing, *The Little Red Book,* Mr. Penick shares how, on numerous occasions, he would have students approach him with the same question. They would ask, "How do I get out of the hazard?"

Penick, being a wise and gentle soul, would smile knowingly and respond, "The first thing we need to do is learn how not to go in the hazard. Think of it this way. If you want to stop eating fat-filled foods, quit shopping at the bakery—don't go there!"

I believe Mr. Penick's advice highlighted the crux of the issue with empathy and understanding. He knew, from many decades of teaching the challenges and vagaries of the game that we do not have to experience difficulties as often as we do. We need simply to learn how to identify and avoid those troubles, in advance, as opposed to dancing with disaster.

When I first read *The Little Red Book*, I chuckled at Penick's advice. Then I sat up a little straighter in my chair as I realized his words had direct application to my life as well as my golf game. In the process of life, I have found myself in a hazard much more often than not, due to poor decisions of my own making.

Sometimes, visiting the hazard isn't my fault—or so I tell myself. In others, I have flirted with danger, trying to go close, while still avoiding the hazard. There are also times when I have outright ignored the hazard warning signs, gone my own way, and had to pay the price.

I have spent a significant portion of my life wandering—unnecessarily—into life hazards I could have avoided. I find it interesting how ego, self-deception, and just flat out ignoring the warnings can sabotage the best of intentions and lead to time in the hazard, and in some cases even death.

On more than one occasion I have been out on the golf course, in the midst of play, when I heard the ominous rumble of rolling thunder and seen the initial flashes of light in the distance, signaling that a storm is approaching. One would think that when confronted with nature's warning signals, I would immediately move out of the impending danger and head for cover and safety. Yet, to be honest, there is something in me that says, *Go ahead, you've got time to finish your round before the storm strikes.* Talk about ignoring the warnings and dancing with disaster!

(Question: Have you ever been, or are you currently, voluntarily involved, in any activity that could be construed as flirting with the hazard—such as habits, behaviors, commitments, relationships, etc.—in which you know you are dancing with potential disaster?)

As I said earlier, my approach to life for many years was that "I make my own rules!" My thinking, sophomoric from the start, was predicated on the notion that anyone else's rules would be burdensome. I am confident that, had I the privilege of expressing my stance on life (i.e., I make my own rules) to the likes of Harvey Penick, during that period of my life, he would have graciously but quickly addressed the error in my thinking in terms of the game of golf and the game of life.

This self-centered approach to life persisted for many years into my adulthood until it finally dawned on me. I was often the creator of the challenges and hazards into which I had wandered. By applying my own guidelines, and by not availing myself of, or adhering to, wise counsel—I had opted for disaster as my destination of choice.

When that reality seeped into my soul and started to take root, it seemed obvious to me that I would need a better guidebook to follow than my own. At that point, I had to ask the question, "Where could I find a better guidebook for my life than the one I had subscribed to for so many years?"

With that question as my motivation, I eventually turned to the Bible my dad had given me several years before, remembering his admonition, written in the flyleaf of his gift that says, *"Read, heed and feed on it, in good health, profiting immeasurably by what His word has for us all."*

(At this point, I find it significant to note that I fought, for a very long time, the idea that the book I had—by choice—ignored for so many years, my Bible, might be the most wholesome and effective guidebook to avoid many of the challenges I continued to generate for myself.)

I have since taken a serious dive into what Dad's book—my Bible/scripture— has to offer on how to better live my one and only life.

When I finally began to read it, I was captured by its words. They were nothing like what I anticipated. They were neither burdensome nor odious. Who can argue with "love one another as I have loved you"? I found guidelines and targets to shoot for, warnings of hazards to be avoided, and simple directions as to what to do when I found myself in a hazard, regardless of whose making.

In addition, I found relief from the notion that I must take all sorts of odious steps to become acceptable. My Maker's Word said I was already loved and accepted as a treasured child of the Most High God. All I needed to do was embrace that acceptance. Its pages also contained the recipe for joy, in this life and the next, regardless of how many hazards I have been in, or, will experience in the future.

Today, I am humbled and thankful to enjoy a peace far greater than I ever expected as a result of my reading and accepting the promises contained in my Bible's pages. If you are frustrated with the trajectory of your life and frequently find yourself in one of life's hazards, you might want to give the promises of scripture a try. If you don't have a Bible, borrow, or treat yourself to one, and give it a shot.

It might be the best shot you ever take.

Because I am not perfect, I am sure I will continue to find myself, from time to time, in a hazard, whether it be of my own engineering or not. For that reason, I have adopted an emergency escape strategy for that eventuality. It includes:

- Pray first! Our Maker is fully aware of every hazard I have ever been in or will be. For best results, I need his help in moving on from that hazard.

- Assess the situation—What do I need to pay attention to, to get from here to there? (Look for the best exit.)

- Pick your target—What is the intended target or destination of my effort?

- Be honest—When preparing to take my shot/action, understand why I am choosing that shot/action. Look at risk/reward then pick the tool I believe to be the best to use, given the situation—What tool and/or action will it take?

- Rehearse my "swing"—what I need to do. How should it look and feel? What temperament, attitude, and strategy should be employed?

- Take Dead Aim– focus on my target, not the hazards. Don't hold back. Once I settle into position, appropriate execution has got to be the most important thing in my life at the moment. Shut out all thoughts other than picking out the target and take dead aim at it.

- Take my shot – it is the hinge point upon which the past and the future swing. The question is what shot/action will I take? The choice is always mine. At this point, I am in absolute control—or not.

- Accept the results – *Grieve or Glow* – Some of my shots may be great, some will be at least acceptable, while still others will be disastrous. I must give myself space to adjust to what has just occurred.

- Learn what I can – do a quick self-debrief on what went well or what did not, and then assess what is required in the future—*grow*.

- Move on – *Go*. Practically speaking there are no do-overs in golf, or in life. After I catalog what was learned, I have a choice to make. I can either hang on to the past or let it go and set my sights on the future. I can either get stuck or get going. What makes the most sense?

(I think of this process in simple terms—"G3"—"Grieve, Grow, and Go.")

Work for the Practice Range:

◄ What are the hazards in life you find difficult to avoid?

◄ Do you sometimes flirt with these hazards—Perhaps getting a little too casual with things such as behaviors, attitudes, promises, or relationships—getting close but hoping not to fall prey to them?

◄ What reward do you believe justifies flirting with the hazard?

◄ What do you do to avoid those hazards before you enter them?

How would you score yourself in the area of *Focus*?

(Scale: Quite well … Birdie 2; Okay … Par 3; Needs work … Bogey 4; A disaster … Double Bogey 5)

Scorecard

	1	2	3	4	5	6	7	8	9	Out	Total
Par	5	4	4	3	4	4	3	5	4	36	
Yardage	547	409	320	295	363	333	278	454	378	3377	
Score											

	10	11	12	13	14	15	16	17	18	In	
Par	5	4	3	4	4	5	4	4	3	36	
Yardage	498	344	228	329	357	436	340	393	285	3210	6587
Score											

*Harvey Penick with Bud Shrake, *The Wisdom of Harvey Penick: Lessons and Thoughts from the Collected Writings of Golf's Best-Loved Teacher* (New York: Simon & Schuster1997) p. 46

Notes:

Hole #8

Par 5

454 Yards

Who's got your back?

(Trusted Advisor)

I Want a Great Caddie...

I am enamored by the craftsmanship of a great caddie. In fact, sometimes I am more interested in watching a caddie ply his craft than the player for whom he/she is working. Sad to say, however, with the advent of golf carts, GPS availability, course calculators and Range Finders the demand for caddies has shrunken dramatically.

On the PGA Tour, you must have a caddie. How you put that caddie to work is up to you—you're the boss. You can use them simply as your beast of burden to slog along beside you, clean your clubs and carry your bag, or, you can employ them to not only do the heavy lifting but embrace them in a team relationship, as your key adviser and confidant, involved in every playing decision you make as you take on the course for your mutual enrichment—win the prize and share the bounty.

One afternoon a few years ago, while attempting to grab a quick preseason golf fix and a hint of summer to come—I was surfing the myriad of sports channels made available by my internet provider when I clicked on to the latest rendition of the 2016 Sony Open underway at the Waialae Country Club in Honolulu, Hawaii. (Please understand—while it may be sunny and 80 degrees in paradise (i.e., Hawaii)—January at my home address is filled with snow and blustery winds and we are still at least two months away from even thinking about heading to the links. So, for the moment, I was keen on vicariously enjoying the Hawaii setting.)

The image that appeared on my TV screen was that of PGA Tour professional Brandt Snedeker, frozen in post-swing position, watching his approach shot, as it soared toward the 16th green. Just then, seemingly as an afterthought, the commentator said, "By the way, for those of you who follow Brandt Snedeker, you will notice his regular caddie, Scot Vail, is not on the bag this week. He is off the tour recuperating from a debilitating foot surgery. In the interim, Steve Underwood is substituting for Scott as Brandt's caddie."

At this point, you might be asking, "Who in their right mind gives a rat's tail about who Snedeker's caddie is?" Answer: I did. It didn't make a huge difference to me who the caddie might have been, but I would be willing to bet the ranch that it made a big difference to Brandt Snedeker. If he won the tournament, it would net him a winner's check with seven digits to the left of the decimal point—that's at least a million dollars in case you are running out of fingers.

Win a million dollars?

That brings an interesting question to my mind. How do you find a caddie in whom you are willing to invest a million dollars of faith and trust—on short notice? That's got to be a fairly short list to choose from. My guess is you would start looking around for the best in the business that's available at the moment. My next question is what criteria would you use to make your hiring decision? The role of caddie is a big and demanding position. That's a tall order for anybody to fill.

Were I to find myself in Snedeker's position—in need of finding a caddie—here is just a short list of the requirements I might have of my caddie. They should:

Be equipped with a sharp mind and focused eyes, dedicated specifically to my success.

Act as part-time surrogate mom—empathy is huge—be companion, friend, protector, enforcer, crowd control officer (no pictures and please turn off your cellphones) encourager, calming agent, buffer, sometimes spokesperson, and fall guy.

Be clear-headed, self-motivated, dependable, very well versed in the rules, and conscientious.

Have a demonstrable proficiency at reading the wind, weather, sun angle, sight lines, grass/green composition, topography, and geography.

Be part greens superintendent and part janitor.

Be in good physical condition in order to act as pack mule to carry what is in my golf bag, packed full of stuff such as extra balls, gloves, rain gear, umbrella, yardage book, bandages, towels, and range finder along with healthy snacks, juice and energy drinks—and, oh yes, no more than 14 golf clubs.

Be faithful to me, the player, even when I may have momentarily lost faith in myself.

I would need whoever is going to tote my bag to come with a proven record of dependability. That is to say, the desirable candidate would be someone, for whom I do not have to set an alarm, is punctual—if not early, and be appropriately prepared with proper equipment in tow. I would want to know if they have a track record of doing the whole job—I would be disinclined to engage an individual for whom it is their first rodeo.

Part of the job description would be the necessity to scope out the course before each round, know the current pin placements as well as the best leave for each shot, and always have the distances readily available. Most importantly, I would want a sense that they would know how to read me, when to encourage, when to provide constructive input, when to talk, and when to remain silent.

The game of golf is a marvelous symphony involving a team of three distinct, yet beautifully blended, entities. Those entities include:

1) The player—"the boss"—who executes the play and is ultimately responsible for the results brought forth by the entire team.

2) The "inner caddie," the inner thoughts and tugs that drive the decisions and behavior of the player. In addition to physical skills, one must apply a cadre of mental skills and character traits. A partial list of those inner caddie traits includes memory, logic, interpretation, patience, honesty with one's self as well as with others, flexibility, knowledge, trust, finesse, and attention to detail. It is the job of my inner caddie to assemble all of this headwork and course management data into a cohesive logical format and deliver it with maximum impact for me—the boss—to consider.
(Note: I have chosen my words very carefully here, to indicate that I, the player—up until the moment I have pulled the trigger on my swing—have the opportunity to choose what advice I will follow and what I will ignore or override.)

3) The "course caddie" who brings to the table all of the elements previously described above, along with varying levels of influence depending on the moment.

It is embarrassing and sobering to note that far too often I choose to ignore, or worse, veto the advice of my caddies—both internal and external. I say this because I have found that this sad practice of vetoing the wisdom of my caddies leads to excursions into folly, which in turn set a course in the direction of eventual disaster. It's just a matter of time, whether on the golf course or in life, until I find myself in a hazard or worse, out of bounds. I have the scars of experience to prove it. Was it the great philosopher, Forrest Gump, who once said, "Stupid is as stupid does"?

We have all the information we need to make intelligent, informed decisions about each shot, right? Perhaps. But the question is not whether or not I have the right information available. The question is, "What do I do with that information?" Just because the information is available does not mean I am willing to take it in, much less act on it.

To demonstrate the value of listening to one's caddies—again, both "inner caddie" and "course caddie"—let me take you through an example of what can happen when one chooses to override the counsel of those caddies.

This example comes to us courtesy of PGA Tour Professional Phil Mickelson— at the time, winner of three Major Championships—the 2004 Masters, 2005 PGA, and 2006 Masters. He was competing for his fourth major. (He has since gone on to win his third Masters in 2010 and the 2013 Open Championship, as well as the 2021 PGA Championship, for a total of six Majors thus far in his career.)

The U.S. Open...

The setting is the 2006 U.S. Open Championship, being contested on the famous Winged Foot Golf Club in Mamaroneck, New York. Phil had taken several weeks to study the course and made more than one visit to the venue spending many hours meticulously identifying the best way to play specific holes. He was once again feeding data to his inner caddie for later use in those crucial moments that would determine whether he would win or lose the tournament.

When tournament time came, Phil played well for the first three days and into the backside of the fourth and final round, remaining among a small field of leaders hemstitching back and forth to the top of the leaderboard. As late as the 14th hole of the 4th and final round, Phil had a two-stroke lead with four holes left to play in the tournament. All he needed, to win the U.S. Open, was to par the last four holes: a feat not that unreasonable in that he had played these holes for a total of one under par over the first three rounds of the tournament.

Phil, however, had hit only two fairways with his driver all day, and they had been on the front side. Then on the 16th hole, he carded a bogey. Now the field got tighter—a two-stroke lead had been whittled to one stroke. He parred the 17th and, stepping to the 18th tee, he needed only to par the 18th hole to capture his fourth major title.

Walking on to the 18th tee, he quickly surveyed the situation. Then, seemingly ignoring his inner caddie, he reached for his driver, a tool that had basically deserted him throughout the day, placed his ball on the tee, took his swing position and pulled the trigger. His ball, in mid-flight, seemed to get a mind of its own, charting a highly undesirable course to the left of the fairway. It caromed off the champion's tent and eventually came to rest amongst the trampled grass and hardpan well off the fairway, with a huge tree obstructing a clear shot to the green.

What would Phil do next?

For his second shot, he selected a three iron, intent on carving a shot around the big tree and on to the green. While this shot choice had a nominal chance for success, the words of caution—the best way is the safe way—resonate from the inner caddie of most players' who find themselves in this predicament.

In other words, "take your lumps, bump the ball back to the fairway, and give yourself a shot at par. If you par, you win. If you bogey, you tie and go into an 18-hole playoff the following day.

Taking his stance, with the entire golfing world watching, Phil unleashed his 3 iron and scored a direct hit on the big (did I mention *big*?) tree he was trying to miss. As his fans murmured, he walked the 25 yards to his ball.

Now with the offending tree close at hand, Phil changed strategies and hit a 9 iron over the top of the pesky tree. The shot missed its intended mark, instead landing in a greenside bunker, creating a crater in which the ball stuck.

Phil's shot out of the bunker would be his fourth and his last chance to save par and win the tournament outright.

His fourth shot—a wedge—went past the pin and stopped in the fringe grass surrounding the green, still a substantial distance from the cup. He could still win if he sank his fifth shot to tie Geoff Ogilvy, and then beat him in the playoff the next day. Unfortunately, it took Phil two more strokes to get the ball in the cup. He walked off the course with a double bogey 6, losing the tournament by one stroke.

In one agonizing hole, he went from being on top of the leaderboard to the depths of despair and self-deprecation, uttering those memorable words "I can't believe I did that … I am such an idiot."[7]

Of course, it's not true. Phil was not and is not an idiot. What he did is common to many of us. He just happened to do it on a world stage with literally millions of people watching. He proved that he was human and subject to making decisions that in retrospect, like the rest of us, he wished he hadn't made.

Retrospect is a wonderful teacher, isn't she? The reality is that either Phil did not hear or did not listen to his inner caddie advising, "Caution, this is not the time for heroics." As painful as this experience was for Phil, it is a vivid and expensive example of the cascading consequences that can occur when we choose not to listen to and follow the advice of our inner caddie.

The Bigger Picture…

A major theme to be constantly aware of in golf is that it is a thought driven game, filled with a multitude of decisions and actions that drive the outcome of one's participation. It is in no way a reflex game. The same is true of life. In both areas, I am ultimately responsible for the decisions I make and the actions that ensue as a result of my decisions.

My thinking follows that if it is helpful to have a great caddie when competing in golf, it ought to be helpful as well to have a great caddie for my life to help me make more informed decisions.

---

7   ArmchairGm, 18 June 2006 <http://www.armchairgm.com/index php?title=%22I_am_such_an_idiot%22>

I believe that life is more fruitful and enjoyable when I incorporate the counsel of trusted advisors to provide input to the decisions I eventually make. I believe my decisions are better formed when I watch, or get good advice from other experienced people I trust. That's why I am mindful and careful in my selection of those I choose as trusted advisors in my life.

The question is, "Where do I find a great 'life caddie' ... one who is eminently qualified to provide great guidance in all aspects of my life?"

First I need to know what I am looking for, which in turn should tell me where I need to look. So, what characteristics should my life caddie have? I have determined that they should:

- Be wise and knowledgeable regarding all aspects of my life.

- Know my every strength and weakness.

- Be with me twenty-four hours a day, seven days a week.

- Show me an honest picture of who I am regardless of who I think I am.

- Provide counsel that is the best available anywhere and be 100% trustworthy.

- Always have my best interest at heart.

- Not be pushy or obnoxious.

- Be able to teach me the life lessons I need to learn.

- Act as my internal compass, pointing to what is right in every situation.

- Be my personal friend, companion, and in difficult times my personal comforter.

When I look back over my wish list, I find it is far-fetched, self-centered, and impossible to fulfill. But the beautiful truth—the good news—is that such a life caddie does exist. He is available to each of us. His services have already been prepaid and are free to each of us. I personally enjoy his company daily.

He is completely conversant with every facet of my life. He is with me 24/7. He never takes a day off. He provides me an honest mirror even when I don't want it. I confide in him with full trust that he will not share my confidences. His advice is always right—always. He always has my best interests at heart. He is never pushy or obnoxious. His guidance comes with an unbelievable gentility and He always shares the truth with love.

He is always on hand to teach what I need to learn. He acts as my internal compass pointing to what is right in every situation. He has become my personal friend, companion and when necessary, comforter. He does not withdraw or go into a pout when I ignore his counsel although I am sure it saddens him. And talk about loyalty, he is commissioned to never leave me.

Who is this guy who has become my life caddie?

He is the Holy Spirit—of God the Father, God the Son (Jesus), and God the Holy Spirit fame. He moved into my life the moment I decided that God had a better plan for my life than I had for myself, including a Savior that erased my troubled past and provided a bright path to my eternal future. He fits my desires to a T, and then some.

When God the Father put in motion his plan that his son Jesus should pay the price to bring onboard anyone who chooses to believe, He knew that we would need constant counsel to live in a new and better way. Therefore, in his plan, he designated the Holy Spirit to act as comforter, counselor, and teacher (a life caddie) to anyone who chose to accept his grace and live their life according to the teachings of His Son, Jesus Christ.

To put the beauty of God's plan in very personal terms, I have been given the promise of living forever in Heaven with the Creator of the universe. For the rest of my remaining years in this life, I have the privilege of being coached by a member of the original construction trio that brought our universe into being. My challenge is to continue the practice of following the guidance of my life caddie. The rewards are priceless!

Most of us have goals in our lives and to reach them, we must practice paying attention to our inner guidance system. Like a high-performance racecar without a steering wheel, we will fall short of our goals without great guidance. The factors that separate those who finish well from those who don't, in golf and in life, are first of all the quality of the caddie and then the continued practice and discipline of listening to and following the guidance of that caddie.

Work for the Practice Range:

◄ Have you ever chosen to ignore/veto the wisdom your inner caddie?

In Golf? Yes/No

In Life? Yes/No

◄ What were the situations and what were the consequences?

Situation in Golf:

Consequences in Golf:

Situation in Life:

Consequences in Life:

◄ What did you learn from those experiences?

In Golf:

In Life:

◄ Who's got your back? Could your inner caddie benefit from having an ever-present life caddie?   Yes/No

If you would like to employ my life caddie as yours, He's yours for the asking. He has plenty of space available for additional clients. All you need to do is ask; He is constantly listening. Your request might go something like this:

"Father God, I open my life to you. Please come in and provide the guidance you would like me to have. My commitment to you is that I will do my best, with your help, to follow that guidance. Thank you for your grace and generosity and your gift of life with you forever."

(Include today's date to mark the occasion, if you like) _____

How would you score yourself in the area of ***Trusted Advisor***?

(Scale: Quite well … Birdie 4; Okay … Par 5; Needs work … Bogey 6; A disaster … Double Bogey 7)

Scorecard

	1	2	3	4	5	6	7	8	9	Out	Total
Par	5	4	4	3	4	4	3	5	4	36	
Yardage	547	409	320	295	363	333	278	454	378	3377	
Score											

	10	11	12	13	14	15	16	17	18	In	Total
Par	5	4	3	4	4	5	4	4	3	36	
Yardage	498	344	228	329	357	436	340	393	285	3210	6587
Score											

Notes:

Hole #9

Par 4

378 Yards

The "Transition"...

(Prepare)

One of the benefits of focusing my writing attention on the subject of golf as a metaphor for life is the conversation I get to have with people who have different interests or lenses on the subject. Those interests run the gamut from utter ambivalence to complete fascination. Each individual has his or her own unique perspective or take on the subject.

One of my more recent conversations on the subject was with a long-time friend of mine—an admitted avid golfer—Rick Marchiori. During that conversation he said, "Hey, I've got a great idea for a chapter in your book. How about writing on the subject of the transition?" Then he added, jokingly, "And if you do, be sure you give me credit for the idea."

I was shocked and more than a little embarrassed at my initial internal reaction—my self-talk—to Rick's suggestion. (But, because confession is good for the soul, allow me to share my first thoughts.)

When he proffered his idea, with the words hardly out of his mouth, my first thought was not *what a good idea*, but rather, *back off, bud! This is my project, my sweat and tears, my thoughts and my energy. You want a voice—write your own book!* I'm not proud of those thoughts. They were unloving at best, and they certainly did not express any appreciation on my part for his idea. (Sounds like an impetuous, spoiled child, doesn't it?)

Understand, my self-talk was going on behind a face frozen in a smile, doing my best trying to disguise my inner feelings. It wasn't until later, having left our conversation and heading home, that the realization of my unfairness and pettiness began to show its ugly head. His suggestion was relevant, beneficial and on point with the topic. I just didn't want to share the limelight with him. I knew then, that my internal responder, my soul, needed a change of direction.

Little did I appreciate, at that very moment, I had just been given a very personal example of the importance of paying attention to a needed transition in my life. It was then that I began to chuckle at myself and be genuinely thankful for Rick's suggestion.

My hat's off to you Rick. It was a great idea.

As I write this, sitting in close proximity to Lake Michigan and approximately 30 miles due west of Chicago, we are in the midst of what, to me, is one of the most welcome geophysical transitions of the year. We are leaving winter behind with its cold winds, snow, frozen lakes, trees barren of their leaves and lawns covered with dormant grass the color of straw.

Simultaneously we are welcoming in the first vestiges of spring, announced by small buds appearing on our tree limbs that will soon open into beautiful green leaves. The skies are getting warmer and daylight lasts a little longer each 24 hours. Small blades of mint green grass have become more prominent, and the crocuses are pushing their heads up through the soil to salute the sun. Spring and new life are upon us.

And ... golf season is here! Hooray!

For the next seven to eight months we will be treated to the sweet aroma of freshly mown grass, immaculately manicured fairways and greens arranged in a beautiful montage of shapes and sizes: all for us to share, enjoy, and be challenged by.

(CAUTION! From one who has enjoyed the game of golf my whole adult life: do not let spring exuberance override good sense!)

In anticipation of getting in a few early season rounds, I was able to go out to my favorite golf course this week to get in some practice swings. After a four-month winter hiatus, I was presented with a rude reality. While my mental game is still sharp—meaning I think I know what my body should be doing—the body is confronting me with a different reality through the language of stiff joints and aching muscles.

It—my body—has another year under its belt and it is letting me know things will not be quite the same as they were last year. The truth is my body is continuing its transition into senior mode—something I need to pay attention to and include in the calculus of my game. (To be honest, the same message has been delivered to me at about this time of year for the past several seasons.)

As a result, I was reminded that it is going to take more than just a few practice swings to prepare for an enjoyable season on the links. This realization has drawn me back to review the basics of good, fluid, swing mechanics, which I now understand need to include paying careful attention to the transition at the top of my swing—something I had never even considered before.

Cautioned by others that I "should be paying attention to the transition", and, it being something I had never considered in the past, I thought it appropriate to get a better handle on what "it" is. To be assured I wasn't on a wild goose chase, I decided to research the Internet for some good advice on the subject. I had no idea how important that split second (i.e., the transition) is to the execution of a good golf club swing. When I did an Internet search for "Golf – The Transition," to my overwhelming surprise—thinking I would be presented with perhaps 10 to 20 information sources—I was greeted with over 2,750,000 entries describing and discussing an event that takes place in a millisecond. My question at that moment was, "how can anything that happens in a mere millisecond generate so much thought and discussion? That's a lot of entries!"

Rest easy—I did not visit all 2.75 million websites. I did, however, get a general idea of *what* the transition is and *why* it is important. Here is what I found:

What is the transition?

It is that millisecond of time in the golf swing sequence when one changes (transitions) the direction of movement of the golf club, from the backswing to the downswing. Acting as an igniter, it unleashes a controlled explosion of energy intended to propel the golf ball from its current resting place to its next resting place.

In that millisecond, maximum available tension in the body is harnessed and translated into energy, making its way from the hands, through the club grip, down the club shaft into the club head, whereupon that energy is transmitted, via collision of the club head face, into the golf ball.

Why is the transition so important?

Any misdirected tension or energy lost en route to the golf ball is of no use in the swing, and the ball flight will stray from its intended target. To get that millisecond of transition right, on a routine basis, takes a significant amount of mental and physical practice.

Needless to say, "I'm not there yet!" It will take some dedicated practice and possibly the assist of a good mirror to help me learn to successfully execute the transition properly on an ongoing basis.

As I prepared to share my thoughts on the transition, it became immediately obvious to me that the subject of transitions is a huge topic!

With that thought in mind, I gave my friend Rick a call and asked him, "What thinking prompted you to make your suggestion that I focus some of my attention on the transition? What do you mean when you say the transition?"

His first thoughts focused on the golf swing stating, "No golf swing can be completed without executing a transition."

Then, as we talked, Rick mused, "The need to pay attention to appropriate transitions is not the sole purview of the golf swing."

> This is a point on which we totally agreed. We reflected on the fact that we must transition from one hole on the golf course to the next ...
>
> ... each hole requires transitioning to a fresh set of requirements to play it successfully
>
> ... to play each hole requires transition through a range of club selections to finish the hole
>
> ... we transition from shirtsleeves and sweaters in fair weather to foul weather gear during times of storm
>
> ... on we went

As we chatted, our scope widened to include the bigger picture of life in general. We noted that the existence of the need for transitions has been with us since the dawn of time when darkness became light and night turned to day. Adam had to transition from being single to having a woman in his life. (A significant transition, would you not agree?) Ever since that time man and woman have been challenged as to how to effectively navigate the vast array of transitions life demands.

During our discussion, my mind flashed back to the first big transition I remember experiencing in my life.

I still recall, with crystal clarity, the summer between my sophomore and junior year of high school. The year was 1961, and I was sixteen years old—going on seventeen in six months—and it was finally my turn to learn how to drive. Having watched two older brothers go through the process over the previous three years I had witnessed, firsthand, the new liberties and opportunities that arrived along with a driver's license. I could hardly wait to take the wheel.

(Forget the fact that stapled to that license to pursue new liberties would be a new set of responsibilities as well. That realization wouldn't sink in until later.)

Through that summer, on into the fall and early winter, I took the required driver's education class, got my learner's permit, and practiced my skills, first with my Mom and then my dad. At that time in my life as a budding young teenager, it seemed like a tediously long process just to learn how to accelerate, steer and brake—what's so hard about that?

Then came the day when I officially became a licensed driver. My very first licensed solo driving experience lasted all of five minutes—a trip to the local grocery store, less than a mile away, for bread and milk so my mother could make French toast.

I remember getting into my dad's car, adjusting the driver's seat to just the right position, checking both the rearview and side mirrors and noting the gas gauge. My heart was beating just a little faster than normal as I turned the ignition key and the engine roared to life—oops, just a little too much accelerator in the start.

Then, moving the steering column shift lever into reverse and grasping the steering wheel at the prescribed 10 and 2 o'clock positions, I could sense the car beginning to move backward from our drive into the street. I don't know that I can adequately express the glee I felt as I realized I was legally driving a car, all by myself.

In my mind, I had just transitioned from a schoolboy to young man. It seems so small now, but back then it was my transportation to the future. It was also the beginning of an era of my life in which I chose to believe that I made my own rules— a decision that almost had catastrophic consequences, due to my arrogant stance. (More to follow on that at another time.)

While I will make no attempt to generate an exhaustive list of life's transitions, I believe it could be useful to tease out a few sureties and possibilities we will face:

- Birth – At that moment we cease being fully dependent on our mother for everything, including breath. We slide into life independent of the womb and commence breathing on our own—a life-changing transition.

- Life – From birth to death we experience ongoing transitions—the growth of millions upon millions of body cells and the death of same—second by second, minute by minute, hour by hour, day by day. Some of those transitions are invited while others are endured. Life can be snuffed out in a second but it takes a lifetime to transition to one's full maturity.

- Seasons of life – From infancy to childhood, puberty to adolescence, adult to full womanhood or manhood on to senior citizen status each season is fraught with beginning and ending transitions.

- Career – Starting with no interest or care, one transition's through a spectrum of life-defining decisions as to which occupation or profession to follow—often requiring multiple iterations.

- Marriage – is a commitment to transition or join together two single people in a binding covenantal oath of love, fidelity, and support. This is likely, for most, to be one of the more trauma filled transitions in life, as newly marrieds step into the challenges of maintaining their own individuality while they function as a couple.

- Divorce – is the transition from married status to single, through the official termination of the covenantal marriage vow. From firsthand experience, it is one of the most excruciating transitions in life. It challenges the veracity of one's views on every aspect of life. Transitioning to new solid ground can be painful, time-consuming, and filled with doubt.

- Death – is the final and unavoidable transition between life and lifelessness, between this life and what's next. It is a transition we all must face.

Of all the transitions one can face and experience in this life, I believe death is the most important. The stakes are high and, depending on whom you listen to, we will not have the opportunity for a mulligan or do-over. Therefore it seems to me that it makes sense to do everything in my power to *prepare in advance* for that guaranteed millisecond of transition.

The jarring truth is that we each have the opportunity/privilege to choose the trajectory of our final transition from this life, through deaths doorway, into the next reality, *before* it's our turn to transition.

I think of it this way: In golf parlance, I don't wait until after I take my shot to figure out where I want my ball to go. It is obviously too late! I make my trajectory and positioning plans, after careful consideration, and then pull the club from my bag that I believe will provide the trajectory and end result I desire. And then I take my shot.

Please don't let the point be lost here. I make my shot and club selection <u>before</u> I execute my shot in anticipation of achieving the desired outcome of my swing.

Question: Why would I take any less care and preparation in selecting the trajectory of my transition into the next reality than I do preparing for my next golf shot, especially when my casualness is destined to lead to a less-than-satisfactory result?

The default position—i.e., not choosing my trajectory before I transition (die)—is to automatically choose darkness outside the presence of our Maker forever. Why? Because God paid the price—via His Son's death on a cross—for our admittance to his presence and sent us an RSVP invitation to join Him eternally. Failure to accept his invitation before we pass will result in refusal of entrance into His presence at the door.

"God so loved the world that he gave his one and only son that whosoever believes in him shall not perish but have eternal life. For God did not send his Son into the world to condemn the world, but to save the world through him." [8]

One Final Question...

What transition trajectory will you choose before you traverse that millisecond of your passing into the next reality, and what advises you to believe your choice is a good one?

Work for the Practice Range:

◄ What is the first significant transition you can clearly recall in your life and what makes it significant?

◄ Have you ever been caught short by not making preparations for a transition? Y/N

◄ What were the circumstances and consequences? (Please describe)

◄ What imminent transitions are you facing in your life? (Please describe)

---

8   John 3:16–17 (NIV)

◄ What preparations have you put in place for those transitions? (Please describe)

◄ What preparations have you put in place as to where you plan to reside when you transition to the next reality? (Please describe)

How would you score yourself in the area of *Preparing?*

(Scale: Quite well ... Birdie 3; Okay ... Par 4; Needs work ... Bogey 5; A disaster ... Double Bogey 6)

Scorecard

	1	2	3	4	5	6	7	8	9	Out	Total
Par	5	4	4	3	4	4	3	5	4	36	
Yardage	547	409	320	295	363	333	278	454	378	3377	
Score											

	10	11	12	13	14	15	16	17	18	In	
Par	5	4	3	4	4	5	4	4	3	36	
Yardage	498	344	228	329	357	436	340	393	285	3210	6587
Score											

Notes:

Lunch At The Turn...

Story time...”The Ultimate Tee Time’

I have fond memories of my early days as a golf enthusiast playing almost every Saturday, weather and season permitting, at the Battle Creek Country Club, where my then father-in-law, Glen Johnson, was a member. The routine was quite predictable. We would arrive at the club about 8:45 a.m., proceed to the locker room to change into our golf shoes and appropriate clothing for the weather, being sure to leave our street shoes outside our locker as a sign to the locker room attendant that we would like them shined while we were on the course—being an ex-military guy it was an amenity of which I was extremely fond.

From the locker room, we would proceed to the pro shop, check in for our pre-arranged tee time and meet up with our playing partners—usually a couple of Glen’s buddies or his customers. Once through the introductions and small talk we would head to the practice green, conveniently situated adjacent to the first tee, where we would practice our putting to work out the bugs in our stroke until we were called to the tee.

I loved the casual elegance of this well-choreographed process as a precursor to getting our game underway. Once out on the course, it usually took us between an hour and forty-five minutes to two hours to play the front nine, which would have us reaching the turn just in time to be able to enjoy the lunch buffet set up in the club Grill Room.

Being somewhat new to life at a country club I was struck by the beautifully carved meats and cheeses, freshly baked bread, fruits, salads, and the bountiful array of pastries just waiting to be consumed. Were you to have looked into my eyes at the moment we walked into the room, I am sure you would have seen them sparkling with delight.

Not only was the food great, the pace of the day was such that we could actually relax and share meaningful conversation and many delightful stories. There was no hurry to get back to the tee. The day was set aside for golf and camaraderie, and both were important.

Had I the opportunity, the following story is one I would have shared at the turn:

My dad was first among the three most influential men in my life. He introduced me, and my three brothers, to the game of golf—although he personally did not like the game; it took way too much time—it was a way of spending quality time with his guys.

A true patriot, he proudly served our country during World War II as an Engineman in the U.S. Navy, attached to a PT Boat squadron, operating out of the Republic of the Philippines. Two decades later, two of his sons would volunteer to serve—one in the U.S. Navy and one in the U.S. Air Force, during the Vietnam era. And continuing the family tradition, one of his grandsons served in the U.S. Navy, supporting our efforts in the Middle East in Operation Desert Storm. All said, Dad set the tone and led the way. (This is a heritage of which I am extremely proud.)

Dad was a principled man. What amazes me—in retrospect—is that he lived a life that reflected his beliefs and yet never once insisted that I must believe as he did. As I described in the forward of this writing, on one occasion, when my life was terribly out of balance and careening out of control, he dropped everything else that was going on in his life, and flew 1800 miles to rescue me from myself and sat quietly by my side for three days, listening as I unloaded a life destined for early destruction.

Throughout those three days he demonstrated and extended to me true selfless unconditional love in ways I still draw from today. His patience and love in the moment initiated a lengthy recovery—mentally, physically, and spiritually—for which I will be forever grateful to him.

(Was Dad a saint? No, but he did provide a role model I could relate to and emulate.)

I did not begin to realize what a central figure Dad was in my life until the late 1980s, some 25 years after I left the family nest. A close friend of mine had come to visit on the heels of losing his father. During his visit, we reminisced and shared fond memories of his dad and the sense of loss we felt. That visit instilled in me an urgency to prepare emotionally for the inevitability of my dad's passing. Shortly thereafter I made up my mind to pro-act to that inevitability and determined to approach him with a very personal request.

I didn't approach him right away. But over the next several months that seed in my soul began to take root, became a tug that persisted, grew to an urging and finally like a sprig of grass breaking through the cement, blossomed into a full-blown undeniable desire. I didn't realize it then, but in retrospect what I really wanted was for Dad to leave me something only he could give, something I could take anywhere and cherish always. I wanted for him to leave me a piece of his heart.

I tried to put myself in his shoes and think what might mean the most to him. What would he want to pass on to me? The thought of his strong spiritual convictions immediately came to mind. I knew that throughout his life, Dad had embraced, and tenaciously hung on to, a set of spiritual beliefs founded in what he had learned from years of studying his Bible and its practical application to his life. He had chosen to let those spiritual beliefs guide his behavior, to the best of his ability, throughout his adult life.

It appeared to me that his beliefs had a value of the highest order. What more could I ask to hang on to than something that had meant so much to him throughout his life? Finally, I decided to act on that desire and make my request. One afternoon, in the early fall of 1989, I picked up the phone and called him at his home in Arizona.

(I didn't realize I was asking him to minister to my soul. How does one ask for that?)

After some pleasantries and family chat we got to the heart of the matter— no pun intended. I tried, as best I could, to explain to him the importance of my request. Not able to find just the right words, I clumsily blurted, "Dad, I would like you to buy me a Bible" (pause/silence ... I could almost hear the beat of his heart as he heard his long wayward son ask for a Bible).

Breaking the momentary silence I continued, "Not just any Bible but one you would like me to have now, and after you are gone. I have only two stipulations. First, it must be able to fit in my briefcase so that I can take it with me when I travel. Second, I would like for you to write to me, in the front of that Bible, any particular thoughts or advice you would like me to carry with me after you are gone."

A few months passed and in the winter of 1989, I received a package in the mail from Arizona. I opened it quickly, sensing that it was most likely the Bible I had requested. To my delight, it was and I immediately opened it to the flyleaf to drink in what he had written. It said:

> 29 December 1989
> Scottsdale, AZ

> Larry:

> The selection of this particular version of Bible ("The People's Parallel Edition") may not be totally to your liking, and in that, I must confess my own preferences. In scanning, I find many good points, i.e., the scriptures themselves; the handy paraphrase version (King James Version/Living: see Prologue for *The Living Bible*); the footnote network; a brief but meaningful topical index; a subject (topical only) concordance; 6 maps keyed to biblical subject and reference.

As an editorial aside, when I got to this point in my reading of what Dad had sent I am humbled and embarrassed to say that I was marginally disappointed. I'm kind of a touchy-feely, heart-on-my-sleeve kind of guy and my guess is that I expected some kind of gooey, perhaps even sappy, comments I could carry around and maybe even weep over from time to time.

Up to this point, his writing hit me as some kind of engineer's specification sheet, a fact that should not have surprised me considering that he had been a design engineer for over thirty years.

It felt like two ships passing in the night. I was expecting one kind of message. He was sending me something entirely different. I don't know what I was expecting; I just knew that what I was reading was not it! This is my dad for goodness sake! Shouldn't he, of all people, be able to intuit what I really need even when I can't elucidate clearly my desires?

In retrospect, I now understand that I had my fathers confused. Out of ignorance, I was expecting a prescience of my earthly father that only my Heavenly Father possesses. Continuing to read, however, and setting my own impetuous nature aside, my heart commenced to soften and his words began the ministry so essential to my soul. With great precision and simplicity, he laid out spiritual mile markers like breadcrumbs to mark the trail for me to follow that have been so precious to him and would, if I chose to follow them, lead me home. (L.G.)

What can I say? My mind/heart is one small sea of warm emotion as we send this Book your way. Warm, in that there is so much natural pleasure in giving, and emotional, to realize again how blessed we are to now share the blessings inherent in its reading and assimilating, and through new or reminded understandings. May I proffer a selection or two, which have recently come to bear more weight?

David's credo: Psalm 119:11 "Thy Word have I hid in my heart that I might not sin against Thee."

Or, one of my favorites: Isaiah 26:3 "Thou wilt keep him in perfect peace whose mind is stayed on Thee, because he trusteth in Thee."

David again: Psalm 19:14 "Let the words of my mouth and the meditations of my heart be acceptable in Thy sight, O Lord, my Strength and my Redeemer."

And more recently: Psalm 46:10 "Be still and know that I Am God: I will be exalted among the heathen, I will be exalted in the earth."

I invite you to read and heed, feed on it, wear it in good health, profiting immeasurably by what his word has for us all.

Some snacks:

1 Thessalonians 2:19, Titus 2:13, Hebrews 6:11, Colossians 1:5

See you there!

> With Love,
> M. L. Galley

Shortly after receiving my dad's gift I began to dig into its pages and discover for myself what it had to say. It was during this time of discovery that I began to legitimately question the content of my beliefs, only to find the cup empty. That discovery (revelation) motivated me to begin doing my homework and take into account the Apostle Paul's advice to "look around", which in turn lead to the formation of the bedrock spiritual convictions I hold on to and cherish today.[9]

For me the circumstantial evidence became overwhelming and I have chosen to stake my eternal life on my belief, based on my personal observations and experience, that there is an intelligent designer, God. The evidence for believing there is a God is overwhelming. While I cannot physically see Him, the evidence of his existence is everywhere. For me, it would take a much greater leap of faith across the divides of understanding to connect an evolutionary process that is supposed to have somehow produced life from non-life and order out of chaos.

Having accepted the reality of a God so immense in intelligence and power that from outside of time and space he planned and put into place this entire

---

9   Romans 1:19–20, <u>People's Parallel Bible</u>, Tyndale House Publishers, 2005

universe it also became obvious to me that the God of the universe is also intimately acquainted with its minutest detail. My Bible, in Jeremiah 29:11, says that God has a plan specifically for me in his overall scheme of things and that it is a good plan, not to harm me but for my benefit.[10]

With that encouragement, I decided to place my trust in the Creator. By accepting the forgiveness Jesus died to provide me, and accepting Him as the Leader of my life, I am comfortably assured that eternal life with the Creator of all things has already begun for me.

As all of these new revelations were beginning to take seed in my heart I experienced a need to express to others what has so graciously been divulged to me via my Bible and my protracted time spent on the golf course. So in 2001, I began to put my notes and thoughts together and write, not knowing whether anyone would have an interest in what I was being led to share.

In the process of preparing to write my first piece, I pulled out all the requisite writing accouterments I thought I would need, including my Bible. For reasons I cannot explain to this day, I decided to read the inscription my dad had sent for the flyleaf of my Bible. I must confess I felt very little new emotion than from the first time I had read it ... then I looked again.

There it was! It had taken him hours and hours or perhaps even days of agonizing soul-searching and a whole page of warm-up verbiage to share what he really wanted to say. He had searched his memory, his heart, and his scriptures. Out had come some wonderful references to live by and passages he had embedded deep in his soul. But somehow there was still a need to seal the deal and share, one more way, what was really on his heart all along. I can imagine, as a dad with my own paternal desires, the lump in his throat, the pounding of his heart and the tears that must have filled his eyes as he wrote and then underlined those three words:

"<u>See you there!</u>"

In those three words, he sent an undeniable message to me that I will tenaciously hang on to for the rest of my days. In three short words, he was able

---

10   Jeremiah 29:11, <u>People's Parallel Bible</u>

to compress a lifetime of learning, belief, and faith. He conveyed everything that his life stood for. He had given me his entire heart. In those three words, he said with crystal clarity "I know I am going into eternity with God. If you want to be with me in eternity this is where I'll be. (He was referring to Jesus comment to his disciples—You know where I am going and how to get there."[11])

What I value most about his challenge to me is that he was given the wisdom to discern his heart's desire and transmit it to me in a way that I could hear and embrace. It was a challenge, an invitation and it was presented in a manner as casual as making a tee time to play golf with an old friend. He didn't preach or plead. He understood we all have the God-given gift and responsibility to make our own decisions about where we will spend the hereafter. He simply and eloquently said, "I would love for you to share this place with me. We don't have to say goodbye. Here's the Map. Trust the Map. Follow the Map.

<u>"See you there!"</u>

---

11   (John 14:4 (NLT)

Hole #10

Par 5

498 Yards

"Gabilicity"

(Integrity)

"You can be forgiven a lot easier for mistakes than for excuses."

– Larry Galley

Golf, around the world, was intended to be a self-monitoring game. That's what makes it unique in the world of sports—no umpires, field judges or referee's to watch for and call infractions—the initial intent of the game was to depend on the integrity of the individual to self-monitor and levy whatever sanction was required, without external monitoring.

I am expected to play by the rules with honesty and integrity regardless of whether anyone is watching or not. This phenomenon is brought to the forefront every time I play the game. Will I be honest with myself and/or others or not? It is one of the factors that allow me to admire the game so much.

Back in the early 2000s, I had the privilege of working in the men's clothing department of an upscale department store. On one particular occasion, while reorganizing the merchandise displays, in wait for the next customer, one of my work co-workers approached me, knowing I am a lover of golf, and unexpectedly began to vent.

The first words out of his mouth were a vehement blurt ...

"I hate cheats."

Curious about the obvious burr in his saddle I asked him, "What's up with that? What do mean you 'hate cheats'?"

His response took me a little off guard when he added, "I hate people who cheat when they are playing golf."

Knowing a bit about his extramarital activities, because he was openly vocal about his weekend exploits, I pressed him on the subjects of honesty and integrity and the potential contradiction between his stated pique with cheaters on the golf course and his weekend behaviors, asking, "You don't seem to have much use for cheaters on the golf course, right?"

"No!" he replied emphatically.

So I asked him, "Well, what is your take on people who cheat on their spouses?"

After a short and rather uncomfortable pause, he said, "That's different!"

Being somewhat bemused at the transparency of his double standard I looked at him, eyebrows raised in surprise, and asked, "How do you square those two positions?"

Not having expected the question, he wrung his hands and shuffled his feet for a moment or two, trying to come up with a legitimate rationale for his dual standard. He then responded with a "c'est la guerre" tone in his voice, "That's just my Gabilicity!"

In the context used by my co-worker, "gabilicity," was his way of describing *a middle ground between right and wrong*. In fact, his use of this expression was an attempt to camouflage behaviors he knew to be inappropriate and avoid taking responsibility for them.

It has struck me that this nonsense, made-up word, "gabilicity," covers a swampland much greater than my co-worker's usage of the term. The damages, spiritually, emotionally, physically, and economically, caused by the application of this philosophy are incalculable. The word, in the context used, attempts to put a fuzzy, comfortable blanket of acceptability over a plethora of less than savory behaviors including, lying, deception, and infidelity to name a few.

Aside from being an attempt to create a space between right and wrong where none exists, it is an attempt to dress sin in saint's clothing. It strives to make the despicable defensible and perhaps even desirable. Finally, to put this smarmy, out-of-focus descriptor into golf parlance: it attempts to define an area, neither in nor out of the hazard. In life, emotional pain, lawsuits, possibly prison, and even eternal darkness are predictable outcomes of its players.

The phenomenon my co-worker described, as his gabilicity, is alive and well, not only on the golf course, self-monitoring notwithstanding; it permeates our society. An impeached president reframes the use of the English language to make room for his lying and behavioral indiscretions, industry chieftain's attempt to explain away fraud, while celebrities of different stripe set their own moral compass, until a light is shone on their behavior. All are sad testimonies of the extent to which this nonsense invades and infects our society.

This whole gabilicity thing appeared on the scene long before golf came on the horizon. We must go all the way back to the genesis of humanity to find our first example. The narrative of Adam and Eve is very insightful.

My Bible indicates, in the early chapters of the book of Genesis, that after God created Adam and Eve, he placed them in the Garden of Eden with this caveat:

"You may freely eat the fruit of every tree in the garden—except the tree of the knowledge of good and evil. If you eat this fruit you are sure to die" (Genesis 2:16–17, NLT).

A loose paraphrase, using golf terms would possibly read:

Then God said, "Look, I'm giving you this entire course to play on and you can veg off any of the trees you like. But do you see that big fruit tree between the ninth and tenth fairways? Don't go near it and don't eat its fruit—it's poison! It'll kill you."

On the heels of God's specific instructions, Satan appears on the scene as a talking snake, introducing our first recorded incident of gabilicity. He convinces Eve that life would be better if she ate the forbidden fruit. So, against her better judgment, she ate the fruit and encouraged Adam to do the same. Immediately, they both realized the magnitude of what they had done. They had disobeyed God on the only issue on which he demanded their obedience.

When God questioned Adam on the matter—here comes the gabilicity— he quickly tried to get out from under the issue by blurting, "Eve—it was the woman YOU created that made me do it." Eve, when questioned on the matter responded, "It was THAT SNAKE that made me do it."

(In both cases the projection—gabilicity—is that "I am all your fault," and, as a result, I should not be held accountable.)

It was as if Eve, ignoring all warnings, stepped to the tee, took a mighty swing and, BAM—hit the ball smack into the out of bounds area. Fully aware of the risk, and God's admonition to "keep it between the lines", she let her desire for the forbidden override God's direction and ate the fruit. Then hoping for safety in numbers, she teed up a ball for Adam and encouraged him to try the shot. He did, his experience was the same, and sure enough, the consequences were immediate, painful (psychologically), and eventually deadly.

Notice Adam's first line of defense, "Yeah, I hit the ball out of bounds, but it's not my fault. She made me do it!" He didn't have the courage to say, "God, I chose to eat the fruit and I'm sorry."

Instead, he pointed a finger at Eve and did a classic duck and cover (gabilicity). He couldn't stand knowing that he was ultimately responsible for his own behavior and that he was wrong. Remember, he had eaten from the Tree of Knowledge of Good and Evil that meant he now knew what was right and what was wrong.

"It's not my fault." Really? What do you think the odds are that God deals in technicalities when it comes to matters of intent or right and wrong, which He can so clearly see?

Ever since Adam and Eve, we have tried to downplay it when we hit a ball out of bounds (sin). We try anything we can to reduce the penalty of owning up to it. First we hit the shot out of bounds and then we try to hide or mask our actions with excuses.

In essence, what we are doing is attempting to carve out that middle ground—gabilicity—between truth and untruth by telling half-truths to justify our behaviors. Half-truth, by half-truth we nibble away at our integrity, credibility, and self-respect.

(I find it sad and convicting, that at the very moment I am striking the keys to write these words, I find myself looking for words to soften the blow to my self-image.)

Here are just a few examples of the insidiousness of gabilicity:

Whiffed...

Have you ever whiffed a shot—swung at the golf ball and completely missed it—and then, with or without the burden of other players watching, chosen not to count the swing?

The gabilicity: "It was just a practice swing. I didn't intend to actually hit the ball on that swing. Besides, I don't want to put an extra stroke on my scorecard for something as stupid as a whiff. After all, it's just a game."

The reality is that I want to be a better player than I really am. And now this whiff is testimony to my own klutzy actions, not to mention the added insult and injury of having to self-report that stupid extra stroke on my scorecard.

In or Out ...

Have you ever hit a shot from a lie that is questionable? You knew deep down inside that it was out of bounds and was subject to a stroke and distance penalty. It was close enough, however, to be questionable, should anyone challenge your decision. So, you declared the ball position to be on the line, which meant the ball was considered to be in bounds, and played your shot without carding any penalty strokes

The gabilicity: "Hey, the lie was questionable, so I gave myself the benefit of the doubt. The course Superintendent should have established clearer out of bounds markings. If it's questionable, I am going to assume the benefit of the doubt falls to me. What's wrong with that? Besides, we had a five-dollar 'Nassau bet' on, and I wasn't about to let my partner down. And you know, everybody else is doing the same thing!"

(Notice here, if you are strident you must be right ... or so you might believe.)

The reality here is that, sometimes, I get my priorities confused. Ego and Integrity get set on a collision course and Ego prevails. I don't want to pay the price of being at fault for possibly losing the hole and having you, as my partner, think less of me for it. So, for the moment, winning—which will feed my ego—supplants Integrity as my higher priority. Some would call this gamesmanship. I call it gabilicity!

The Padded handicap...

Have you ever padded your handicap—assuming you have one? You know, only post your higher scores when establishing or updating your handicap status, knowing full well that in so doing you give yourself an unfair advantage come tournament time. Some think this practice allows them a more competitive position during tournament play because they come into the event disguised as a player of lesser skill who might just get lucky and play over his head during tournament play.

The gabilicity: "I know for a fact 'everyone' does it. Don't be naïve! You don't know these people like I do. They all do it. It's expected. If I don't, I don't stand a chance."

The reality is that it is CHEATING! It places winning above honesty and ego above integrity. It also disengages honest self-monitoring, which is one of the key components in the games of golf and life. It provides key testimony regarding my character. What makes it worth it to cheat?

Let's go to the business/life side for a bit and look at a few samples:

The Speed Limit...

Have you ever pushed the speed limit, kind of eased on up beyond the speed limit, but just short of what you believe will net you a speeding ticket, only to get pulled over anyway? (I have.)

My gabilicity: "Officer, I wasn't that far over the limit and besides, I was just keeping up with the traffic. After all, isn't there a certain 'grace zone' that you guys recognize? There were people passing by me like I was standing still. Why don't you pick on them?" To which the officer replies, "Here's your ticket sir. Hope the rest of your day gets better."

The Expense Account...

Do you know of anyone who has taken liberties with their expense account? By that, I mean used their expense account to pay for things that were not legitimate business expenses or created documents to represent business expenditures when in fact those documents were not factual?

The gabilicity—usually offered, with certain vehemence or bluster—"Hey, you don't know how many times I have eaten the bill and the company never knew it. There have been many times I didn't charge the company for legitimate expenditures. Besides, their guidelines are way below what a decent meal costs. I am not about to be a 'Big Mac diner.' And have you seen what it costs to take a client to a decent golf course these days? It's not cheap and the company doesn't cover all the expenses. My allotment for expenses isn't nearly enough! So, of course, I sometimes turn in 'seasoned' reports to recover some of my 'real' expenditures. That's only fair."

The raw reality is that—no matter how I might try to justify my behavior—to turn in a false expense report is serious gabilicity. In fact, it is attempted theft, grounds for dismissal and even prosecution for fraud. The first clue that this might be inappropriate behavior is the defensiveness welling from within. If everything were on the on the up-and-up, there would be no need to defend the actions

My final example in this sampler is painful to even bring up. But it is so pervasive I would be remiss not to. (Remember these are all examples of gabilicity, the supposed netherworld between right and wrong.)

An Affair of the Heart...

Have you ever cheated on your partner in your heart? Have you ever looked at someone and just wished you could be with him or her instead of, or in addition to, your partner, even for a moment? There is a term for that desire. It's called lust.

The gabilicity for this desire is one of denial. Can you hear yourself saying: "Wrong! I have merely admired this person from a distance. Nothing, I say again, nothing has ever happened from my just looking! I love my spouse. Yes, when I see a particularly attractive person, I can sometimes feel my prop spinning and my heart beat a little faster. But the person I am looking at doesn't know I have had these feelings and thoughts, so how can that be wrong? There is nothing wrong with looking as long as you don't touch! Right?"

The term wandering eye has a negative connotation for a reason. When my fantasies begin to form I have begun the journey away from innocence. Regardless of whether anyone else knows it, I do. And with that journey will come the high probability that I will polish up my own line of gabilicity. My affections will be split between what is and what might be. I cannot give full service and affection to my legitimate relationship and harbor those fantasies.

My partner is shortchanged. Guilt and potential stress and relationship issues stand in the wings, almost sure to follow.

Jesus had this to say on the subject: *"You have heard it said that you must not commit adultery. But I say, anyone who even looks at a woman with lust has already committed adultery with her in his heart."*[12]

I, and perhaps you, wrestle with occasional bouts of gabilicity. We are all human and thus fallible. We momentarily disregard our moral compass and chart our own course, not fully appreciating the depth and breadth of the potential pain-filled consequences. We ignore the risk, take the shot, and cut the corner. If the shot does, in fact, fly out of bounds or into the hazard, we instinctively want a mulligan or a do-over and out pops the gabilicity.

In essence, we want to hit 'til we're happy—however long it takes—without suffering the consequences of our actions. When the inevitable does occur, we do everything we can to avoid paying the piper. And nowadays the piper is usually a lawyer.

An affair of the heart is anything but harmless. Wisdom says, "You may not be able to avoid seeing, but you can avoid the second look. Don't take the second look!"

I am amazed and frustrated at how often I am tempted to ease into the supposedly safe harbor of half-truth and excuses, i.e., gabilicity. Every day I fight the battle of choosing between right behavior and something less. Even more frustrating, I live in a society that applauds and romanticizes living in the middle ground between right and wrong. I am barraged, daily, with a multitude of media campaigns urging me to live on the edge.

A perfect example of this "taste the forbidden pleasures of life without <u>consequence</u>" message is captured in the ad campaign to encourage tourism

12   Matthew 5:27-28 (NLT)

in Las Vegas, Nevada, that boasts, "What you do in Vegas, stays in Vegas." This ad is a shameless enticement for me to indulge myself in limitless pleasures, supposedly without consequences.

Really? What about my conscience? It goes everywhere I go. Regardless of whether anyone else knows, or finds out about my behavior, I know, and my Maker knows. This ad plays in the darkest corners of the gabilicity playground. To buy into and respond to its invitation would cause significant damage to my soul.

As I think through this whole idea of gabilicity and all it portends for my life, I ask myself, *Why do I do it?* Why do I sometimes take the low road of lame-brained excuses and half-truths instead of simply taking the high road of honesty and good character?

My honest answer to the question is that I don't want to pay the penalty strokes that honesty and integrity demand. Regrettably, sometimes I massage the notion that there must be some kind of recovery shot to execute that will allow me to avoid the consequences of a situation my behavior has generated.

What I know, but misplace in my mind from time to time, is that the God who loves me sees all that I do. I fail, in the moment, to appreciate the value that God places on honesty, and, because I can't see Him or hear Him speaking to me audibly, I am deluded into thinking perhaps *He won't notice me ... just this once.*

I forget that God, who promised, "I will be with you always," is the same God who is my Savior for all situations. He wants the best for me at all times, not just for a future time but also right now ... today. He is immediately available to give me the strength, courage, and determination to honestly handle any situation. I don't need any gabilicity!

I do need to listen to the spirit he has planted within me and heed that guidance. The fairway is the best place from which to play good golf; God's way, simple honesty, is the fairway of life and the best place from which to play my life.

My personal experience is that regardless of the situation, whether it is on the golf course or in life, temptations will come. Satan delights in hitting me in my weak spots when I least expect it. In order for me to maintain any sense of good character or integrity, it is essential that I discard gabilicity as a go-to option. When I keep that in mind, the air seems much fresher and life is much more enjoyable.

For several years now, I have been searching for ways that will prepare me to be less susceptible to gabilicity and its consequences. And, while I am not immune to its reach, I have found four things to be helpful:

1. Inoculate Daily

Just as some people must take daily insulin shots to keep their body chemistry in balance, I must have daily real—dedicated, not on the fly—contact with God to maintain my integrity and honesty. I ask God to speak to me, in whatever form necessary to get my attention, open my eyes and ears to see, hear and do what is right.

2. Be Aware

Temptations will come. I don't know where, when or how they will come but rest assured, they *will* come. I must be vigilant to recognize the assault.

3. Be Prepared

When the temptation comes to deploy gabilicity, I must remember my ABCs:

   A. Delay *action* long enough to act advisedly. Take a deep breath and ask, "What is true here?"

   B. *Be* mindful of the moment. Listen to the tugs of my conscience and the Holy Spirit that are my internal voice—my life caddie—signaling the right thing to do, regardless of the consequences that might accrue.

   C. Muster the *courage* to act appropriately to those directive promptings.

4. Practice Daily

One final thought ...

Sometimes I flirt with the out of bounds markers. Flirting with the out of bounds markers is to flirt with disaster. On the golf course, it's just a game. In life, it can have life or death consequences. It's always my choice ... honesty, integrity, and good character or gabilicity?

These will be your choices too. What will you decide?

Work for the Practice Range:

◄ Do you have any areas of your life in which you occasionally slip out to the Gabilicity playground? Yes/No

◄ If yes, describe a situation where you opted for Gabilicity over a more savory course.

◄ What actions might you take to decrease the amount of time you spend on Gabilicity in your life?

How would you score yourself in the area of *Integrity?*

(Scale: Quite well ... Birdie 4; Okay ... Par 5; Needs work ... Bogey 6; A disaster ... Double Bogey 7)

Scorecard

	1	2	3	4	5	6	7	8	9	Out	Total
Par	5	4	4	3	4	4	3	5	4	36	
Yardage	547	409	320	295	363	333	278	454	378	3377	
Score											

	10	11	12	13	14	15	16	17	18	In	
Par	5	4	3	4	4	5	4	4	3	36	
Yardage	498	344	228	329	357	436	340	393	285	3210	6587
Score											

Notes:

Hole #11

Par 4

344 Yards

82!

(Problem Solving)

"The score we post is determined by the choices we make."

– Larry Galley

It wasn't working!

A few years ago—approaching the end of the golf season—I had a rather disturbing epiphany regarding my game. It occurred to me that I had been trying to be everyone but myself on the golf course. In my mind's eye I had concocted a vision of my being one part the swashbuckling Phil Mickelson, one part the precise and masterful Tiger Woods (in his heyday), equal parts of loquacious Lee Trevino and comical Chi Chi Rodriguez, all wrapped in the congenial cloak of Payne Stewart. Yes, I was trying to stuff all five personas into one golfer ... me!

(You might say I was full of myself, trying to be someone I am not.)

I began to realize that my golf game had become a convoluted mess that neither I nor anybody else could recognize. I had become so busy trying to emulate the prowess of others I had lost any sense of the natural swing I once possessed—however good or bad. It had gotten to the point where it was difficult to recognize any golfer within. What made the situation even more pathetic was that I could not conceptualize what might happen if I started being myself—by that I mean, working on my swing with the gifts God granted me in my uniqueness.

Yes, there were core concepts I needed to pay attention to. And yes, there were substantial deficiencies in my play when compared with the people I was trying to emulate. The lunacy of my behavior, however, lay in the fact that never, in my wildest imagination, had I ever considered becoming a professional golfer. I had always played for the love of the game and the joy I derived from the experience and yet, even as a rank amateur, I saw myself as needing to *appear*, at least on the surface, more professional.

Something had to change!

For the record, I am a wannabe golfer with over 50 wonderful years of golfing experience at this writing, and I have played courses of varying beauty, uniqueness, and difficulty on several continents. And I still fantasize about playing more beautiful courses in my remaining years. I have never played a stellar game, but at one point in my golfing career, my scorecard registered scores in the mid-eighties, which is a significant distance from the triple-digit scores I have carded more recently. (Age and ego have a way of taking their toll.)

With all of the above as preface, I'd like to share the events and results of a four-month journey of discovery and revelation that occurred a decade or so ago.

Accepting reality...

At that juncture in my golfing career—understand I use that term loosely—I had strayed so far from a recognizable golf swing that I had no idea how to stem the unrest within, generated by my decaying skill sets and an aging body. I was lost. To make matters more challenging, when I would swing a golf club my body hurt from my nose to my toes, which ought to tell you I was doing a whole lot of things wrong in my swing.

Make a decision...

At that time, I was confronted with choosing whether to put away my clubs and become a full-time spectator of the sport, or, rise to the challenge of reestablishing a level of play with which I could be satisfied and thus bring back to me the joy of the game. To put it another way, should I give up the game because my body had deserted me, or, should I take on the game with a new passion, determined to learn the skill sets required for me to play a decent game with my body in its current form? (Read: How honest would I be with myself?)

To play or not to play, that was the question? (Thank you, Shakespeare.)

Inspiration...

Everyone needs motivation: it is the fuel that energizes movement. During that same summer, in the midst of my personal angst of to play or not to play, I chose to read Tracey Stewart's biography of her husband, the late PGA Professional, Payne Stewart—not surprisingly titled *Payne Stewart: The Authorized Biography*. At one point in the book, Tracey relates the story of a family conversation the Stewarts were having in preparation for Payne's upcoming 1998 tournament schedule. It read:

"Aaron, our nine-year-old, is as straight forward as Payne. In comparing Aaron to himself, Payne often said, 'The apple doesn't fall far from the tree.' When we were discussing how Payne might be able to play fewer tournaments in 1998, Aaron cut right to the chase. 'Just play better, Dad, and you won't have to play so much.'"

"Payne cracked up at Aaron's blunt honesty and his simple solution. 'Ooooookaaay, I can do that,' Payne said as he leaned back and laughed. Sometimes the obvious answer is the best, although not always the easiest."[13]

---

13   Tracey Stewart with Ken Abraham, *Payne Stewart: The Authorized Biography*, (Nashville: Broadman and Holman Publishers, 2000) 222

For some unknown reason, that phrase "just play better, Dad" took root in my imagination and I began to think that even I, with my own set of foibles and swing challenges, could improve my game. And, if that were true, I should jolly well get on with the process of improvement and jettison any notion of giving up the game I have loved for so many years.

The more I thought about young Mr. Stewart's comment the more sense it made to me. It was concise, precise, and to the point: "Just play better." The question was, how? How indeed!

Identify and commit...

One Saturday morning in mid-July, with Aaron's mantra exciting my soul, I declared to my wife that for some time my golf game had been in disrepair—a fact she made no effort to dispute—and that I was going to set out to change that situation. I explained my philosophy of how I might realistically attain a score of 82. I then put a stake in the ground. I projected that by the end of the current golf season I fully expect to legitimately card that score. (Keep in mind I had not shot below 100 in the past three years—that's 18 strokes I was looking to drop from my best score in three years.)

Upon hearing my rather optimistic projection, my wife smiled warmly at me and said, "That sounds like a great goal; it should be a wonderful learning experience."

That's "wife talk" for, "Sounds good to me, I'll listen to your words but I will watch your feet." In other words, don't just tell me about it, go make it happen and then I'll celebrate with you.

Establish where you are...

There is an old navigation adage that says, "Wherever you go, there you are." My first hurdle was to do an honest assessment of the state of my game—to determine where I was with the state of my game. Initial practice and recent scorecard history defined my current situation. I was confronted with a rude awakening. I was nowhere near the golfer—coldly and effectively defined by my performance—I thought I was. I had become, in essence, a legend in my own mind.

Look ahead, not back...

Next, I had to start practicing with a vision, purpose, and commitment! At the moment I had no practice regimen. Previously, when I did practice, it was merely to hit a bucket of balls on the practice range and spend a few minutes on the Putting Green—hardly what anyone would call dedicated practice. There was no doubt some things needed to change—the question was what things?

(At this point, I had to draw down on a piece of advice a writer friend of mine shared with me years before, when I asked him, "When you sit down to write and you don't yet have your thoughts in good order, how do you start?" He looked at me with a knowing smile and said, "Once upon a time .... Just start writing, go from there, and refine. You'll figure it out.")

Just Start...

With that thought in mind, I went to the practice range and began to practice and figure it out, one club at a time, with no particular strategy in mind. I learned I was not hitting any of my shots as far as I thought I should. (This was important information to know because the distance I could comfortably hit each club with confidence was and is one of the primary determinants in my club selection for each shot.)

I had lost a full three clubs in yardage—meaning I was currently hitting each of my clubs roughly 30 yards shorter than I had in the past. In addition, I was having problems with my accuracy. It would make no difference how far I hit the ball with a particular club if I needed a hunting dog to find it when it came to rest.

These maladies existed in part because of poor swing form and also due to advancing age as well as body changes that were occurring as a result of some recent surgery. What a surprise! (Note to self: insufficient exercise, poor swing mechanics and body changes can, and will, take their toll.)

Do the necessary...

Each day I worked on a different iron, hitting what seemed to be a multitude of balls, to establish a new baseline of numbers (yardage/distance) I could reasonably expect to achieve from each club, while at the same time continuing to work on my swing mechanics.

It was frequently hot, muggy, and often times windy during those long hours. But what was emerging was worth it. A new sense of hope was blossoming. I actually began to believe I could achieve and perhaps surpass my goal. With that new hope emerging, I began to practice with greater fervor.

There were seemingly endless hours of tedium as I hit shot after shot, long after I wanted to quit, trying to extract whatever learning I could from each swing. Many times I would get to the point where I would tell myself, "There, I've got it," only to, on my next swing, lay back a piece of sod so deep and wide it could pass as an extension of the Panama Canal.

Over the summer and into the fall, as my practice progressed, I was encouraged that perhaps my goal would become a reality and not just a dream. It took center stage in my soul and, I began to perseverate on it, dream about it, and chase after it with a new vigor. I was committed to doing anything I could to reach my goal. It was during this time of heightened excitement and tunnel focus that I had to come to grips with a new revelation:

Not everything one learns about golf, and subsequently about life, is learned on the course.

Celebrate each day...

As I continued to practice, what began to emerge was a player who hit the ball decently and played within himself. However, the road was neither easy nor straight. This required that I become reacquainted with the necessity to celebrate the little successes of each day—a process that became a steadying influence along the way.

I started to look not only at my swing but my headwork and the tactics I applied to each hole. I paid greater attention to the conditions present at the moment (wind, rain, temperature, height of grass, lie, and more). I actually started to read the course (situation), not just the greens—an activity that had escaped my attention in earlier years. I discovered that where I hit the ball was every bit as important as how far I hit it.

Looking back over my years of life and golf, the truth is clear to me. No one can give me a day I have lived or a round of golf I have played back. Equally important: no one can take away the joy I have experienced from both. My challenge is to hold the best of both in my heart and pass on what I can to others.

Not a race but a Journey...

Growth in my life and my golf game are both dependent on my keeping an open and receptive mind for what I can learn next. My joy in both comes not from the score but from the Journey.

To this day I have yet to reach my target score of 82. My game, like the stock market average, never travels in a straight line. Some days I am pleased and on others my score is not so good. The good news is that regardless of whether I am playing my best or something less, as long as I have breath, I can learn from the moment and press on for the goal.

Author's Note: In the process of reviewing this chapter I was presented with an interesting surprise. This piece, quite unintentionally, mirrors the problem-solving model I have employed for over 30 years in addressing situations large and small in my life.

Give yourself some quiet time to honestly process the items I have suggested. The time you invest now may have a significant impact on your future.

Work for the Practice Range:

◄ Establish where you are. Describe WHERE you are right now, with regards to your current frustrations. What does it feel like or look like and what situations do you find causing those frustrations? (Keep in mind: you have no way of establishing what changes are necessary until you have a firm handle your current situation.) Write down your current situation.

◄ Identify *WHO* or *WHAT* might be motivating your need for change.

◄ Describe *WHY* you feel the change or changes you listed above are necessary? (Remember, if you understand the *WHY*, you can handle any *WHAT*.)

◄ Look ahead, not back. Are you sitting at the back of your boat looking aft? Or are you at the bow, looking out to the future to see where you are going? What do you see in front of you? What's your vision? What is it you want to accomplish? What is your goal? Write it out.

◄ Celebrate each day along the way. Describe HOW you will celebrate each day on your way to attaining your vision or goal? Finish the sentence "I will celebrate each day in my effort to change by ...."

◄ Not a race but a journey. Describe your understanding of the phrase "not a race but a journey." How does this apply in your golf and life journeys?

How would you score yourself in the area of ***Problem Solving?***

(Scale: Quite well ... Birdie 3; Okay ... Par 4; Needs work ... Bogey; A disaster ... Double Bogey 6)

Scorecard

	1	2	3	4	5	6	7	8	9	Out	Total
Par	5	4	4	3	4	4	3	5	4	36	
Yardage	547	409	320	295	363	333	278	454	378	3377	
Score											

	10	11	12	13	14	15	16	17	18	In	
Par	5	4	3	4	4	5	4	4	3	36	
Yardage	498	344	228	329	357	436	340	393	285	3210	6587
Score											

Notes:

Hole #12

Par 3

228 Yards

" ... Oh no! Hit a Brick"

(Remorse)

I have maintained for years, and iterated in other portions of this writing, that I consider the game of golf and its surroundings to be a marvelous metaphor for life. The challenge is what do I do with the metaphor? Do I listen to the lessons being provided and respond accordingly, or, do I move blithely on, ignoring what the course has to ask or teach? Such was the case a few years back.

The setting was the Barona Creek Golf Club, nestled in Wildcat Canyon, a quiet high canyon valley, just a short distance from Lakeside, California, and roughly 30 miles northeast of downtown San Diego. The air was clear, with visibility hampered only by the mountains marking the periphery of the canyon, and the temperature hovering in the 60s. All said, it was a beautiful day for golf.

We had teed off somewhere around eleven o'clock and it was now mid-afternoon as we approached the green on the 300-yard par 4, 14th hole. The course was in excellent shape, the greens swift but fair, and I was having one of my better rounds.

Given the contour of the green—sloping significantly down from back to front and from high on the left to low on the right—I felt fortunate to have parked my second shot roughly 15 feet to the left and slightly above the cup. While I was glad to have reached the green in 2, I now faced a putt that would break sharply to my right and require a delicate stroke to coach the ball down to the cup, but not past it.

While I surveyed the situation, I was telling myself, *You're in good shape to sink a putt for birdie or at least par.* At the same time, another sense from within was cautioning, *Don't get cocky and get ahead of yourself. Just continue to play one stroke at a time.*

I went through my pre-putt routine—which included trying to read the line my putt should follow, checking the complexity of the downhill slope, as well as attempting to get a handle on approximately how much pace I should put on the putt.

Cautiously, I stepped into my putting stance over the ball, took a breath as I reviewed my calculus one last time, and then putted. At the moment of impact, my sense of feel, and the voices of experience and observation, collided in an explosive message in my head, telling me, *Oh man ... you've given your stroke way more juice than you needed!*

As this blinding glimpse of the obvious was racing through my noggin, I watched—now, with everything moving, seemingly in slow motion—as my ball rolled by the cup with no indication of slowing, while I was simultaneously beginning my trek to the "war room" of my mind, to assess the damage and commence to assemble a recovery strategy. All of this internal commotion was set in motion because of an erroneous message I had sent down the shaft of my putter into the club head and transferred into my ball.

(Note to self: Be careful the messages you send. They may come back to haunt you!)

Can you spell "self-recrimination"?

Experiencing a case of the "stupids," I could almost hear my ball, now out of my control and rolling on its own, taunting me like an impudent child saying, "Alright, I'm going where you sent me, and I'm not stopping 'til I get there, and you can't stop me. I am all your fault! So there!"

In the midst of this little vignette, playing out in the theater of my mind, I heard words of anguish coming from my lips resembling, in a tone of voice, a request for divine intervention: *"Oh no ... HIT A BRICK!"*

This, while my little spheroid, showing no interest in my prayer, ambled on, finally came to rest in a place of its own choosing, some twenty feet beyond and two feet below the cup, as I muttered to myself, *I'll be fortunate if my next putt gets me within 'gimme' range.*

✕

You may be wondering at this point, "So, what does that expression, '*HIT A BRICK*,' mean?"

The loose translation of this prayer/plea, at least for me, is "OH NO! I screwed up. Help! I want a do-over I can't have." In essence, I want a different past.

(Note to self: Not happening! Ugh!)

Usually, when I blurt those words—HIT A BRICK—there are two things going on inside my head and heart. First, I am frustrated and chastising myself for the poor read and/or the poor execution of my putt, the ball following my directive stroke is now out of my control. Second, I am casting up an after-the-fact, futile prayer for a result that is different from the one that is on its way to becoming a reality.

✕

This futile little phrase—HIT A BRICK!—has much greater significance to me than I want to admit. I am challenged to consider how often, in other parts of my life I, metaphorically, putt first and pray later, crying out (audibly or not) "HIT A BRICK!" or words to that effect, hoping for a different result than is now anticipated.

A few examples of this phenomenon, from slight to serious, include ...

... Speeding through an intersection believing the traffic signal is still on yellow, only to be confronted by a flash from the traffic camera indicating a traffic citation and fine will be in the mail shortly—"Oh no! HIT A BRICK!"

... Continuing to flirt with the line between right and wrong, (the list is long, going back to early childhood) functioning under the bogus assumption that there is a middle ground—a gray area—that separates the two, only to find myself damaged and on the wrong side of the line—"Oh no! HIT A BRICK!"

... Having consumed my days, focusing primarily on chasing fulfillment and satisfaction through my career, now standing at the door, watching my offspring as they head out that door into a life of their own, while I stay behind wishing I had spent more time, and paid closer attention to my relationship with them— "Oh no! HIT A BRICK!"

... Professing, to others and myself: "I alone am the master of my destiny and as such I make my own rules. No one decides for me what is right and wrong." Only to find out that this approach is hopelessly egotistical and I am dramatically misinformed—"Oh no! HIT A BRICK!"

Of course, we will blunder and make mistakes, some big, some small, throughout our lives. Reality suggests that we all, from time to time, find ourselves in situations where we want to utter "Oh no! Hit a Brick!" The raw truth is that things do not always go well, regardless of how well we plan.

I suggest wherever decisions or actions are indicated it is always good to remember that now is a perfect time to pray about impending decisions and events. To spend my "now" time praying for the past is futile and frustrating.

How about you? Are you spending your time frustrated and wishing for do-overs, or are you praying first and moving ahead?

This author's confession: Every day, as I sit down at my desk to write, I am confronted with a Post-it Note, stuck at eye level on a bookshelf edge, situated directly in front of my desk, not three feet from my eyes. It reads, very simply:

"Pray First."

While it is a noble directive, I am continually amazed at how frequently, even with that note staring at me, I proceed with whatever task is at hand without giving prayer a thought, until I hit a rough patch in what I am doing.

When this occurs my bent is to retrace my steps, offer an opening "Oops!" to my loving and caring, Eternal Father, and then, banking on His promise that if I acknowledge my screw-ups, He is "faithful to forgive"[14] I then share my concerns with Him and we move on.

Something to chew on...

If you are searching for words to ask for God's help, these offerings might be of some use:

"Heavenly Father, please give me the strength and perseverance to stay focused and on task even when many distractions are begging for my attention. And please infuse in me the wisdom and courage necessary to share what you have led me to share. Thank you."

Now what?

I've heard it said, "Even God can't steer a parked car." My job, once I have prayed, is to step out in the faith that He has provided what I need and get busy! I need to put into practice those things I have respectfully requested—strength, perseverance, wisdom, and courage. The message, to me, is clear:

God has given me the tools; now it's my responsibility to put them to work.

Thank you, Father.

---

14   1 John 1:9 NLT

Work for the Practice Range:

◄ Are you aware of the God-given gifts, talents and/skills you have been given? Y/N (If so list them here.)

◄ Describe a "Hit a Brick" situation you have endured in your golfing experience. *(If you have played any golf at all … you have one. L.G.)*

◄ What could you have done differently, or better, in that golf situation?

◄ Describe a "Hit a Brick" situation you have experienced in the larger landscape of life.

◄ What could you have done differently or better in this life situation

How would you score yourself in the area of **Remorse?**

(Scale: Quite well ... Birdie 2; Okay ... Par 3; Needs work ... Bogey 4; A disaster ... Double Bogey 5)

Scorecard

	1	2	3	4	5	6	7	8	9	Out	Total
Par	5	4	4	3	4	4	3	5	4	36	
Yardage	547	409	320	295	363	333	278	454	378	3377	
Score											

	10	11	12	13	14	15	16	17	18	In	Total
Par	5	4	3	4	4	5	4	4	3	36	
Yardage	498	344	228	329	357	436	340	393	285	3210	6587
Score											

Notes:

Hole #13

Par 4

329 Yards

Passion ... For what?

(Passion)

Passion: Something important enough to draw or drive one across a divide—whether it is a hurdle or abyss, physical, emotional, or spiritual—to get to the desired goal.

Have you ever heard the old vaudeville shtick about the chicken crossing the road?

The routine involves two comics:

The first backhands the arm of the other and asks, "Why did the chicken cross the road?"

The second comic responds, "Well, I don't know."

The punch line, offered by the first, in uncontrollable laughter—"To get to the other side!" (Bah dum bump!)

What brings that shtick to mind is not its lame humor. As a matter of fact, by most people's standards, the joke is hardly funny. No, when I peel back the thin veneer of humor, I find a profound question, one that demands an answer, if I want to do my best: What is it that will entice me to pay the price necessary to go where I want to go or do what I want to do? Or, to put it in vaudeville terms, "What will it take for me to want—and then take the necessary steps—to cross the road?"

I have been facing this question throughout my whole life, sometimes ducking the challenge, and at others, taking it head-on. My guess is that you have too.

In mid-July of this year, I binge-watched the 147th rendition of The Open Championship—a tournament many of us in the U.S. still refer to as the British Open—contested, this time, at the Carnoustie Golf Links in Angus, Scotland. This defiantly bold links course is considered by most tour golfers across the world to be one of—if not the most—difficult links courses they face in the world.

The Open is a tournament that seems to draw out the best of its competitors—and then some—and still requires a bit of luck thrown into the mix. This year was no exception. No player in the tournament had a hope of winning or even surviving the cut—after 36 holes—without a significant driving desire/passion to compete, endure, and emerge Champion of the Year—a title earned by winning the 72-hole contest.

I watched as Francesco Molinari shot a bogey-free, 2 under par, round of 69 and bested all of his opponents by two shots over the four rounds to win the championship and have his name inscribed on the world-famous Claret Jug.

During the closing awards celebration, I couldn't help but wonder, *Do I have, or could I have, that kind of dedication, determination, and desire/passion about anything?*

The answer—for me and for you—is definitely yes! We as newborns arrive with desire/passion hardwired into our being and only we can allow it to dim. Perhaps it's latent or unobservable at the moment, but it is still there.

Think about this. Have you ever witnessed a child on their way to learning to walk? I'll give you my twins, born in 1968, as examples.

One foot somewhat in front of the other, one step at a time, they practiced.

I have fond memories of watching (and helping) our twins take their first steps, and ever so shortly thereafter, their first solo walk. In between those two points were countless finger walks—those rather awkward step-by-step adventures as they grasped my fingers.

I can still feel the squeeze of their tiny fingers wrapped around one of mine as they began working out for themselves this thing called walking. We made progress a step or two steps at a time. Then they began to use anything they could reach to steady themselves.

Finally, after many plops on their backsides and then working themselves back to their feet, they defiantly pushed aside any offer of help and moved out on their own. Their fat little legs eagerly reaching forward, balance questionable and course uncertain, they finally made their way across the room.

Each step was a triumph as they navigated their way on those first walks. The fascinating thing to me is that my little ones did not know that they had goals, that they needed to practice or that they were developing coordination. They did not know they were working on, or developing, the leg strength they needed to walk.

They simply had an undeniable urge/desire to get over there—wherever there was—and they set out to get there on their own. They were willing to do whatever it took—that's passion—to get where they wanted to go. Their seemingly undivided attention—between naps—was to become good at walking. They found ways to use what they had and were unhindered by the things they did not have, they just kept on chugging.

In thinking about those—then infant—rascals in their quest to get from here to there, I noted that they exhibited a cadre of inborn gifts, a partial list of which includes:

- Vision

- Energy

- Perseverance

- Creativity

- Unwillingness to accept defeat

- Focused use of time

- Heart – courage

- Passion – *intense drives or feelings*

This was quite educational to me. Even in their infancy they were exercising their ability to choose and were able to operate with undivided focus. What amazed me, when I thought about it, is that the characteristics listed above are the same as those exhibited in the lives of individuals who seem to be the most successful and perhaps satisfied with their lives.

We all have those gifts residing within us; it's just a matter of using them.

At this point in my golfing career, I am certain that more of my playing days are behind me than lie ahead. I also know that my body is constantly changing as I move into my senior years, and my game these days requires that I employ more brains, due to less brawn.

It's ironic that it took me 50 some years of playing to figure out that brains and brawn relationship thing, but hey, better late than never. Nevertheless, the results have been delightful as I approach the game with a renewed vigor that had been absent for a while.

As an example of that approach and vigor, I have chosen to move forward to use the senior tees—or as Harvey Penick chose to refer to them, "the seasoned tees"—just aft of the forward tees. As a result, I have experienced a new joy of being able to play the game, not merely try to keep up with the young bucks.

(This has all occurred by dusting off and utilizing some of those same gifts I was given at birth, to address "what I can do today," and let what I can't, be "gone with the wind.")

Over the years I have seen golf as a wonderful object lesson that I can borrow from and take to the course of my life as well. The delightful realization that "I ain't dead, therefore, I ain't done," has transcended my golf game and that same sense of excitement has eased into the mainstream of my life as well.

As a result, approximately six years ago, I began to exercise and put to work my delight with words and started to blog. Not sure whether my ideas were worth sharing, I approached the process slowly, with some fear and trepidation that I would make a fool of myself. After all, who wants to read the yammering's of a dusty old unknown golfer on the backside of his given years?

My first efforts at writing were much like my twins' first efforts at walking ... there were many plops on my backside. (It became readily apparent that, like learning to play good golf, writing is not an event but a journey. You acquire refined skills as you dedicate and apply yourself to the process.)

About two years ago I began entertaining the idea of transitioning from blog to book to share my thoughts. I took a hiatus from posting my blog to look into the art of publishing. While significantly more challenging than blogging, I decided to shift gears and create a manuscript for publication.

During the beginning stages of this period of transition, I received an unexpected call at my home in Geneva, Illinois, from a gentleman in Florida. I had no idea who he was or why he was calling. But after a quick "hello" and a few "You don't know me but" pleasantries, he got right to the point, saying, "Larry, I have followed your blog and I sincerely believe you need to be writing more. You definitely have something worthwhile to say."

To say that I was stunned is an understatement. Here was a man who had taken the time out of his schedule and put forth the effort to call a perfect stranger, a thousand-plus miles away, and provide words of encouragement that I never expected to receive.

It was as if God Himself had called and said, "Larry, it's time for you to get off your backside and put to work the gifts I have given you! Got it?"

It took me a while to get through the "Are you sure, God?" phase. But about a year ago I made the decision to actually invest the time, pay the emotional and physical price, and pursue my quest to share my passion, in book form.

Having made that decision I began, in earnest, to get the myriad of notes—three binders full of page after page filled with Post-it Notes—I have been scribbling and saving for the past fifteen years and start assembling them into a readable, and hopefully, embraceable form.

For the past thirteen months, I have spent, on average, six days a week, five hours a day confronting the keys of my MacBook Pro with my ideas, confessions, confusions, and revelations.

To continue this process I have repeatedly had to revisit and draw from those gifts I received over seven decades ago and summon the strength needed to pick myself up off my mental backside, reach forward, balance uncertain, course uncertain and try again until I get there.

I can tell you from firsthand experience, it is taking:

- Vision

- Energy

- Perseverance

- Creativity

- Grit – Unwillingness to accept defeat

- Focused use of time

- Heart – courage or enthusiasm (especially when maintained during difficult situations)

- Passion

My hope is that little by little I will become an ever-better writer, able to communicate what my heart is prompting me to share. I am truly passionate about this sharing.

My reality is that passion, dedication, practice, and repetition are baseline necessities for golf and for a fulfilling life.

A thought to ponder...

I have three friends who are currently approaching, or have recently passed over, the threshold of retirement. They are all in decent health and looking forward to retirement life. When I asked each of them (separately) what they plan to do in retirement, none of them had given any serious thought as to what they wanted to do. The common response was, "I'll figure that out when I get there."

I have shared with each of them, and I will share with you, speaking from experience, "Retirement without drive/passion is a recipe for disaster."

(Remember, you can argue my thinking, you can't argue my experience.)

Passion is the fuel that drives one to do all that is necessary to achieve their purpose.

Noted psychotherapist, university professor, author, and Holocaust survivor Viktor Frankl coined the dilemma "Sunday neurosis"—describing it as "a form of anxiety resulting from an awareness in some people of the emptiness of their lives once the working week is over—or they enter 'retirement.'"

He went on to say, "Some complain of a void and a vague discontent. This arises from an existential vacuum, or feeling of meaninglessness, which is a common phenomenon and is characterized by the subjective state of boredom, apathy, and emptiness. One feels cynical, lacks direction, and questions the point of most of life's activities."[15]

This void, however, can be forestalled or avoided altogether by devoting some significant thought and energy into identifying and defining what you desire to achieve and then pursuing it with passion.

---

15   https://en.wikipedia.org/wiki/Viktor_Frankl)

Warning: the process of pursuing your passion is not a game for the timid! It takes never-ending work, attention to detail, and a dedication to persevere, even when things are difficult.

(Lest you doubt the veracity of this scenario, one of those three friends—the one who retired just a little over a year ago—has gone back to work because he felt, in his words "absolutely lost." This is serious stuff. Don't fall into the trap of waiting until you retire to give this subject significant thought. Denial will only last so long before the pain begins.)

Net/net on the subject, it is healthier to live with passion in my life than to live without.

I will likely be more productive, no matter what my stage of life, happier with myself, and more pleasurable to others, by taking the time to identify and live out my passion.

What about you? Only you know what vision is strong enough to entice you to get out of your comfort zone and do whatever it takes (pursue your passion) to get to the other side. Only you can muster the energy and thought power it takes to identify your actual goals. What is it that really drives or draws you in any given area of your life?

What are you passionate about?

Work for the Practice Range (*Think carefully. Your answers could make a tremendous difference in your future.*):

◄ Are there areas in your life where you are "just putting in your time"? Y/N
If yes (above) what can you do to change that?

◄ What areas of your life are you passionate about?

◄ In those areas of your life you are passionate about, what draws you to them?

◄ What passions are driving you to practice these days and how so?

◄ We have a passion for many different things in our lives. Do you have a passion for pursuing and honoring what you say you believe in your spiritual life?

How would you score yourself in the area of ***Passion?*** (Scale: Quite well ... Birdie 3; Okay ... Par 4; Needs work ... Bogey 5; A disaster ... Double Bogey 6)

Scorecard

	1	2	3	4	5	6	7	8	9	Out	Total
Par	5	4	4	3	4	4	3	5	4	36	
Yardage	547	409	320	295	363	333	278	454	378	3377	
Score											

	10	11	12	13	14	15	16	17	18	In	
Par	5	4	3	4	4	5	4	4	3	36	
Yardage	498	344	228	329	357	436	340	393	285	3210	6587
Score											

Notes:

Hole #14

Par 4

357 Yards

"It's Not Fair" ... Who Promised That?

(Fair)

Life is not fair ... why should golf be fair?

– Pete Dye

Did you ever see a golfer (think the GEICO caveman) get all tensed up, in preparation for their tee shot, clamp their club in a wrestler's death grip, and then, just as the symphony of their swing is about to unfold, you see the guy take an extra "rump waggle" that sends his club into a double "octaflugeran"—it's an aviators term for flight aerobatics, don't worry about it—en route to his ball that is perched innocently on its tee?

Sure you have, and I bet you can predict the outcome.

The result of this rather grotesque scene is that our man's ball, having no mind of its own, innocently takes its orders from the club head face and moves down the fairway an awesome 150 yards before exiting the fairway and coming to rest a good twenty yards into the deep rough. To make matters worse his ball is now seated directly behind a huge tree providing him no access to the green on his next shot.

Seeing the situation—he alone has created—you hear him begin to rant, "It's not fair. It's just not fair. These fairways are way too narrow. Even the pros couldn't hit them. The course architect is obviously an idiot. And by the way, mister 'knot head' caddie, why did you ever suggest I use this stupid club for that shot?"

(You might be thinking at this point that perhaps the player under review might be better off taking up another sport ... perhaps peewee golf.)

An exaggeration, for sure, but I am confident, if you have played golf for more than a couple years you have seen some of this type of behavior. As opposed to stepping up and saying "I screwed up," the player lets out a yelp followed by an ego salving blurt, "IT'S NOT FAIR!" The projection being, "I'm a better player than that. It's the course's fault!"

(My sense is that if you're looking for fairness on the golf course or in life, you have come to the wrong venue.)

It seems to me that fair is a highly overworked, overrated, and misplaced concept when it comes to golf ... or life. One of the things I find truly fascinating about both games—golf and life—is that their unfairness is what makes them infinitely fair—unfairness in some way befalls all of us, even our Maker.

Part of God's design is the uniqueness of each of his children. Where there is uniqueness between individuals there will always be inequities. A perfect example of this uniqueness is the differences between male and female. I, being a man, cannot bear children. My wife, being female, has the pleasure and the pain of bearing a child. We are each made uniquely.

Life has its written and unwritten laws, understandings, rules, and cultural mores that provide a skeletal framework around which a society functions. As one moves from society to society, country-to-country, culture-to-culture, or region-to-region, the emotional, physical and legal terrain changes. Is that fair?

In golf, we have a voluminous set of rules to help provide a semblance of order for the game, regardless of where or when it is played around the world. These rules overlay a population of individuals and a terrain of varying complexity and composition, which at any given time favors some and not others. Is that fair?

Consider the following…

In my twenties—some fifty years ago—I could hit the ball a good distance and because of my distance, my ego advised me that it was appropriate that I play "from the tips." (Whether that was good advice or not is certainly an arguable matter.) But something has happened along the way. I've gotten older.

While I'll take older over dead, it does have its challenges. My body doesn't respond to the swing commands of my brain the way it did in my youth. I don't hit the ball as far as I once did. It just isn't fair! One bright spot to this scenario—if there is one—is, because I don't hit the ball as far as I used to, it is much easier to find.

It is generous, and I am thankful for, the rule makers and course designers of the game, who have made playing concessions for those of us who are of an advanced age. Because we have multiple tee boxes, for varying skill levels, I can, if I choose, let go of my ego and hit from the senior/seasoned tees—thank you, Harvey Penick. But I have to ask, is it fair that I have to endure the internal chagrin of swallowing my ego just because I no longer hit the ball as far as I used to?

Sounds like the lament of a cranky old coot, doesn't it?

In terms of fairness let's look at four unique examples (Jake, Lance, Bobby, and Payne).

Jake and Lance…

Jake has an early tee time and steps to the first tee to compete in a tournament under brilliant sunlight, light breezes, and a refreshingly clear blue sky. It is 8:21 a.m. local time. Throughout the round he notices the weather is changing, the winds are stiffening and the clouds are beginning to build in the west. By the time he finishes his round, at 12:05 p.m., the skies are gray, the winds are gusting to 30 mph, the temperature, with wind chill factored in, has dropped a good 20 degrees and rain is definitely threatening. I know, I know … welcome to fall golf in Chicago!

As he is walking off the 18th green, having finished his round, Jake sees his friend Lance, also in the tournament, who is just walking to the first tee for a 12:10 p.m. starting time. Lance will tee off from the same tee in the same direction over the same terrain as Jake did earlier but face entirely different conditions. He will face bone-chilling 30 mile-per-hour winds and a threatening sky. In addition, there is the strong likelihood that his group will not finish their round without a rain delay and, because of that rain, turf conditions will change mid-round, all of which will likely have a negative effect on his score.

Meanwhile, Jake, having posted his score for the round, will be sitting snuggly—or smugly as the case may be—in the clubhouse, enjoying his post-game burger and fries. How fair is that? In the interest of fairness, shouldn't every competitor have to play the game under the exact same conditions?

Answer: No, not in golf and not in life.

Bobby (Jones)...

The story of Bobby Jones is legend. A Georgia son and considered a shining star, Jones took the golfing world by storm. He is most famous for victories in all four major tournaments of his era—The Open and Amateur Championships in both the U.S. and the U.K.—in the year 1930. Throughout his playing career, Jones played in 31 majors, winning 13 and placing among the top ten finishers 27 times.

He then retired to pursue other interests, choosing to devote his time to his law practice and co-designing, with Scottish architect Alistair Mackenzie, the world-famous Augusta National Golf Club. In 1934, Jones decided to invite some of his friends to come and experience his masterpiece of golf course design and participate in a little "friendly tournament."

Out of that beginning emerged what is known today as The Masters. It is the first of four designated tournaments played throughout each year as part of the modern day Grand Slam. The other three "majors" include the U.S. Open, The (British) Open, and the PGA Championship.

Jones continued to play in his own tournament until 1947 when a spinal disease caused his health to fail, eventually affecting both his arms and legs and confining him to a wheelchair, thus ending a brilliant playing career.

Some time after Jones was required, due to his sickness, to give up golf, one of his acquaintances—in a well-meaning attempt to empathize with what he thought might be Bobby's sense of resentment and frustration—lamented in despair how unfair it was that Bobby's disease had taken away his ability to play and enjoy the game he so dearly loved.

Bobby replied, "I tell you privately: it's not going to get any better. It's going to get worse all the time. But don't fret. Remember, we play the ball where it lies, and now let's not talk about this ever again."

Was it fair for the man who had given golf so great a legacy to be sidelined by a vicious disease? Answer: No, but he was.

We sometimes have the luxury to prepare for events, which seem so unfair. On other occasions, we are absolutely blindsided. The latter was the case in this last example.

Payne (Stewart)...

Because of my love for the game of golf and its players, October 25, 1999, stands out as a pinnacle experience in my memory of unfair events in the golfing world. On that day, the nation was advised of a "runaway" executive jet aircraft that seemed to be wandering across the skyways of the United States with no signs of a pilot at the controls. The plane did not seem to be on a projected course. Nor, was there a flight plan registered with air traffic control that matched either the course or the varying altitudes the plane was traversing.

Military aircraft were launched and multiple forms of contact were attempted including radio, hand signals, close aboard flybys, and wing waggles. Every avenue of contact that could be thought of was attempted, while behind closed doors there were nervous discussions about the advisability or necessity to actually shoot down a friendly, wandering business jet from the sky to avoid it crashing into a major population area and killing who knows how many people.

The newscasters following the story were reporting that military aircraft had even tried to get close enough to the flight station of the aircraft to see if they could identify any signs of life. Nothing! We, the nervously waiting public, had been informed early on in this saga that the aircraft had departed Florida, headed for Texas and that PGA Tour Professional, Payne Stewart, winner of the 1999 U.S. Open and a small group of his business associates were on board.

What made this episode so poignant, for me, was that Payne Stewart was one of my personal favorites on the PGA tour. He had flair, panache, and style (remember the Plus Fours and Tam-o'-shanter?). He played with a casual abandon, was described as "a bit of an imp"—my style of guy—and, he had an absolutely beautiful golf swing.

What made him even more endearing to me is that I had heard from various sources that his entire life had recently undergone some marvelous spiritual awakening, which was reflecting positively in his professional performance. Life had seemed to really be coming together for the Stewarts.

And then, 3 hours and 54 minutes after departure—the aircraft carrying Payne, his colleagues, and the flight crew—pierced the surface of the countryside at close to Mach speed, just outside the town of Mina, South Dakota, leaving a gaping hole in the earth as well as in the hearts of all who loved them.

It's not fair! It's just not fair!

Answer: No, it's not … but we still get to deal with it.

Finally, on the subject of fair …

Writer and well-known motivational speaker, Zig Ziglar, would often state this cold truism, "Life is not fair; it (life) just is."

God never promised fair. He promised he would love us always and He gave us this most precious and costly of gifts … choice. God, Maker of all things, responsible for the creation of the universe, loved us so much—His creation—

He gave us—you and me—the unbelievable privilege of choice. He didn't have to, but he did. In fact, He loves us so much that, even though our choices have lead to trouble of our own making—sin—He has given us the privilege of choosing whether we want to be made right with Him and join Him on into eternity in spite of our shortcomings/sin, or, to his devastating disappointment, turn our back on Him and live forever without Him. How fair is that to our Creator?

I made my choice. I dearly want to go into eternity in the presence of my Heavenly Father. I accepted the gift he gave me of eternal life with Him by recognizing and accepting the grace He provided me as a result of sending His Son Jesus, to bear the consequences of my misdeeds (sin) so that I can approach him and live with Him, unblemished by my past. I'm so glad He did not demand "Fair" in my treatment.

Is it fair that God had to send the Holy Spirit, third manifestation of the triune God, to golf courses literally all over the world to get my attention and display the message of his love?

Is it fair that he had to use the arena of golf to establish in me a recognition of the need for civility, order, and honesty, character and how important forgiveness is to my very being?

Is it fair that God had to provide his Son as a living sacrifice to provide me a pathway back to him from my pit of debauchery? Is it fair that I—impetuous child that I am—insisted that He unwrap some of the gifts he had in store for me *before* I would give Him the time of day?

My answer to each of these questions is No! It was not fair, but I'm sure glad He loves me so much that he did all those things in spite of my impetuousness and ignorance.

I wish I had paid attention to the Apostle Paul many years before his words came crashing into my heart in such a way that I could accept and embrace them. He said in the first chapter of his writings to the Romans, roughly 2000 years ago:

"For ever since the world was created, people have seen the earth and sky. Through everything God has made, they can clearly see His invisible qualities— His eternal power and divine nature. So they (we – LG) have no excuse for not knowing God."[16]

How about you? Have you made your choice? Have you taken unfair advantage of God's offer of grace, forgiveness, and acceptance to be with Him eternally or are you still in pushback? Will you spend your eternal future with God or without? The choice is yours.

I am so glad He didn't promise fair.

Work for the Practice Range:

◄ What do you see when you walk on to the golf course? (Beauty, risk, reward, challenge, caution, hazards, creative genius, horticultural splendor, out-of-bounds areas, pristinely manicured greens, freedom of choice, and more.)

Mark the things you see and add your own observations to the list.

◄ What would happen to the game of golf if it had to be fair?

---

16   Romans 1:20 NLT

◄ What would happen if the game of life had to be fair?

(The above questions may seem simple to respond to, however, think them through, and weigh the consequences of fairness in your answers.)

How would you score yourself in the area of **Fairness?**

(Scale: Quite well ... Birdie 3; Okay ... Par 4; Needs work ... Bogey 5; A disaster ... Double Bogey 6)

Scorecard

	1	2	3	4	5	6	7	8	9	Out	Total
Par	5	4	4	3	4	4	3	5	4	36	
Yardage	547	409	320	295	363	333	278	454	378	3377	
Score											

	10	11	12	13	14	15	16	17	18	In	Total
Par	5	4	3	4	4	5	4	4	3	36	
Yardage	498	344	228	329	357	436	340	393	285	3210	6587
Score											

Notes:

Hole #15

Par 5

436 Yards

Today I Hit a Shot Out of Bounds

(Forgiveness – moving forward)

*"It isn't what happens to you, it's your interpretation
of the situation which dictates your response."*

– Stephen Covey

I have been playing golf for a long time now. And during that time I have scattered shots out of bounds all across the U.S., Asia, Europe, Central America, the South Pacific, and the Caribbean. Fore on the right!

I don't like hitting shots out of bounds. Who does? I do, however, love the challenge of a course that tests my capacity and willingness to exercise good judgment and think through each shot before I swing away. A course of this sort challenges my self-honesty and at the same time, shows me how good my game really is or is not, depending on the day. To score well on a course with this type of character is a source of great satisfaction to me.

One such venue resides on the southernmost tip of the Baja Peninsula, just a short Taxi ride to the east of the resort community of Cabo San Lucas, Mexico. The course, Palmilla Golf Club, designed by Jack Nicklaus, creatively incorporates dry desert landscape, foothills of the adjacent mountains and excursions to the ocean's edge where the Pacific Ocean and the Sea of Cortez meld, providing the golfer with an optically magnificent and skill challenging environment.

My favorite hole in this resort setting is #5, on the "Mountain/Ocean course." It is strategically positioned to take full advantage of a natural arroyo. The arroyo is, in reality, a steep-sided dry riverbed populated with cactus, boulders of various sizes, sand and desert scrub brush. This arroyo can quickly turn to a raging watershed during the heavy seasonal rainfall, providing a channel for the rain runoff to reach the oceanfront below.

The teeing area, nestled hard against the right side of the arroyo offers the golfer tee to green yardages of from 401 yards for the more seasoned player, moving closer to 298 yards for the lesser skilled or powerful. The player has no choice but to navigate over this arroyo twice en route to the green.

To me, this hole—#5—is an interestingly designed challenge—beautiful for sure, but also devilish. The right side of the fairway, situated across the arroyo from the tee box, hugs the arroyo's edge as it runs diagonally, left to right, away from the tee, thus providing you with a teasing decision as to how much arroyo you choose to take on. The more arroyo you take on, the more carry your tee shot must have. The penalty for falling short on your tee shot is a trek down into the arroyo for your second, third, and possibly fourth shots in route to the green, which is situated on an island plateau in the midst of the arroyo.

I love this hole. It intrigues me because it requires a peevish dance with decisions, prior to each shot I take. It tests my capacity to exercise sound judgment, common sense, and good play or yield to the foolishness of my ego. It allows me to risk as much as I want—in my quest for the lowest possible score—while keeping in mind the sure knowledge that I will enjoy the immediate consequences of my decisions. It constantly pits my avarice against my exercise of wisdom or the lack thereof.

Have I always played this hole well? I'll not share my scorecard with you, but suffice it to say, I have room for improvement. But, let's move on ...

(Sounds kind of like life doesn't it? I take my shot and then I reap my reward, either positive or negative.)

This hole—upon occasion—brings to the front my ability to let go and move on, or, linger and disintegrate emotionally.

I hit shots out of bounds or into trouble with more regularity than perhaps others—hopefully not as many as I used to—for a variety of reasons. (My brain failed me, I have insufficient skill, my execution was faulty, or the serendipity of things beyond my control stepped in—excuses, excuses, and more excuses!)

More often than I am want to admit, I experience that jolt of adrenaline and distress associated with watching a shot I have launched skyward toward my intended target make an immediate exit, left or right, headed for the out of bounds markers, into a hazard, the water, or simply disappear into the ether, never to be seen again—usually initiated by my poor judgment, faulty shot execution, or a combination thereof.

I am not alone in this. Over the years, I have witnessed a wide assortment of player histrionics. I have seen, and heard, golf clubs "helicoptering" into the distance, launched from the hand of a disgruntled player—as if it were the club's fault. I have heard volumes of profanity, appeals to the risen Savior, screams of anguish, observed steel club shafts broken over a player's knee and seen gestures I refuse to describe, all as a result of anger over bungled shots.

(In life, we might call that sin. In golf, we euphemistically call it the "momentary loss of control.")

On the other hand, I have seen players simply shrug it off, give a quick thought to what needed to be corrected, tee up another ball, and move on. That is not to say that they were happy with the turn of events, only that they did not go ballistic. They merely took in stride the fact that an error has occurred and they won't get the shot over. They embrace the fact that errors are a part of the game. The question is how will they keep those errors to a minimum?

(This is an available choice in golf and in life.)

What makes hitting a silly little white ball to an unintended destination so painful to some of us? For me it is, in part, because I can't lay my misdeeds off to someone else. My manifest behavior did not live up to what my ego tells me is true. Yet I can't turn to my playing partner and credibly say, "It's your fault I hit that nasty shot. I'm taking it over!"

It doesn't work that way. I must take responsibility for my shots, the good *and* the bad, and count *all* my strokes. I hate that accountability stuff!

(Again ... sounds like life, doesn't it?)

The question is, "What do I do when my ball comes to rest out of bounds, or lost in a hazard?"

The answer:

Rule 27-1: If a ball is lost or is out of bounds, the player shall play a ball, under one stroke penalty, as nearly as possible at the spot from which the original ball was last played. USGA *2018.*

This test of skills, wills, and mental toughness are what make golf, and life, such great games. Truth be known, I must confess I have not, and do not, always deal well with this issue—stuff happens. Let me lay out a scenario that is far too common for me.

Picture this scenario—I know it's difficult but please humor me. I have just hit a horrible tee shot, sending the ball flying out of bounds. I now must reload and prepare to take my third shot from the tee—the rules of golf having extracted their penalty—one out, one in, hitting three. Inside, I am burning with a case of the stupids. I call myself all sorts of names that describe what a miserable player I am and what a stupid shot that was!

If I immediately reload and swing—read without taking a moment to gather myself—it is like I have put my foot on my neck and then, with a mighty swing try to fire the ball as far down the middle of the fairway as far as I can, to make up for my errant first shot. Because I have taken no time to grieve or repair, odds are good that my third shot will likely be a poor one as well, lending credence to the well-known and oft-ignored advice applicable to both golf and life … *"Don't let one bad decision or swing be followed by another."*

In essence, if I do ignore that advice, I have, instead of forgiving myself and letting the issue fade, chosen to wallow in loathing and self-pity and ruin my game for several shots to come, which only makes my game worse. How sad is that?

As the decades of my life have begun to pile up, some sanity has set in. I have come to embrace what my first golf mentor, Glen Johnson, taught me. He would watch me flail away for two or three additional strokes trying to extricate myself from a difficult position, created by some previous poor decisions, trying to hit through, over or around trees, out of high-lipped fairway bunkers, from water hazards and deep grass.

And then, while he would never tell me precisely the shot I should hit, he would instead, gently chuckle and remind me "When you get into trouble, the best approach is to knock the ball back into the fairway as quickly as possible and go from there. You'll be much better off in the long run." The basic lesson was "the long route is the shortcut. What looks like a shortcut, isn't**."**

Glen's advice is as valid today as it was more than fifty years ago. To follow his advice, I need to pay attention to three things.

First, I must get over what has happened. As much as I would like to, I cannot take the shot over. I must play the ball where it lies. And, once again, I must acknowledge that I am not perfect. This is not always easy and it takes a little time. I need to let my adrenalin bleed off and common sense return. I need to step away from my shot stance, take a couple of deep cleansing breaths, forgive myself and then turn my thoughts to the next step. In short, I must take time to grieve. According to psychologist, author, and fellow golfer Henry Cloud, "Grief is accepting the reality of what is."

Second, I must review what went wrong, keep my head about me and focus on what do I need to do right. (Focusing on what went wrong and trying not to do it again is a solid recipe to produce further faulty action.) I must insist on learning what I can from each shot, focusing on what I know to be the right swing for the situation. From each bad shot, I have the opportunity to learn. I must learn if I am to grow.

Third, I must move on. I need to go.

Play on!

Try as I might, I have found no successful alternative to this three-step process. To cut it short is to invite trouble. This coping progression has been of great value to me not only on the golf course but in the larger game of life as well.

Sports psychologist Bob Rotella says it all in the title of his book, *Golf Is Not a Game of Perfect.* In my estimation, he should have added to that title "And neither is life!" I know from personal experience that life is not a game of perfect either. I know that I was created perfectly by God for His perfect plan for me. He wired into me a perfect life-swing, custom designed for his purposes.

However, whenever my life-swing—the chosen spiritual, emotional and physical functions of my life—do not replicate the swing model He wired into me, I am likely to end up in the rough, the hazard or even the out of bounds of life. That's when stuff (sin) happens.

Whether by accident or intent, omission or commission, I have hit many life-shots out of bounds and have had to endure the consequences of my behavior. Some of my errant shots have created excruciating pain and devastation, some haven't. Just because I am committed to following Christ's teachings and look forward to graduating into eternity with Him does not guarantee that I will not pull off some incredible blunders along the way.

I don't get up each day and plan how to mess things up—but I do, with alarming frequency, hit a life shot out of bounds or into the rough—i.e., sin. Fore on the left!

When those blunders occur, I know I need to go to the Master, the Creator, the Pro of my life, the One whom I can trust more than anyone in this world and ask, "How did this happen?" Listen, learn, and then humble myself and ask Him to "Please forgive me." On the heels of my request for forgiveness by my Maker, I must, in turn, forgive myself and if reparations are necessary, begin the process. To not do so is like constantly playing out of the tall fescue of life. It is very wearing and self-defeating. Let it go.

There have been times when I have made such a mess of things that I have to let the dust settle, let the pain subside, and the adrenalin abate. I need to grieve. How long this takes can vary. Grief is like that: IT TAKES TIME—maybe seconds or minutes, hours or days. Grief is good for a season but not for a lifetime.

I have found, not surprisingly, that the same three-step process I use on the golf course is applicable to my life. When I hit one of life's shots out of bounds—I know that I have sinned—I feel a sense of grief and remorse. I know I need to admit I was wrong and *ask forgiveness from God, others AND MYSELF*, whatever the case may be.

At this point, I need to take a quick time out to share a piece of personal learning that has taken a long time to come into focus and for me. For years I have understood the significance of seeking and receiving forgiveness from God and others for my misdeeds. It has taken me much longer, however, to grasp the significance of forgiving my self.

I understood how God in his infinite mercy forgave me when I asked. And I understood the necessity of forgiving others. It was the self-forgiveness part that hobbled me. I found myself thinking that God might forgive me, but I would never be able to forgive myself—as if to say, "I know what a miserable wretch I am better than God does, and I am not forgiving me!" (Remember the image of me on the tee with my foot on my neck?)

It wasn't until I began to ponder Jesus' words, recorded in Matthew, that I started to gain a new perspective on forgiveness. In this passage, Jesus had just finished giving his disciples an example of prayer, known as The Lord's Prayer. Jesus then added this caveat:

"If you forgive those who sin against you, your heavenly Father will forgive you. But if you refuse to forgive others, your father will not forgive your sins."[17]

I believe Jesus meant that when God, the Father, forgives me; it is with the clear mandate that I must forgive myself as well. It comes down to this: when God forgives me, I dare not withhold forgiveness of myself.

It is neither healthy nor does it advance God's plan for me to be shackled by un-forgiveness. His plan, through Jesus' death on the cross, was to lift my sins from me *so that* I wouldn't have to carry a load that might be getting in the way of my doing what he wants me to do with my one and only life. He never intended that I should hang on to them. I cannot move on with the plans God has for my life while clinging to the sins of my past.

Once I have grieved—sought forgiveness from everyone involved—I need to check out what I can learn from my mistake, so I can change my behavior in the future. The essential question is how can I grow from the experience?

Think of it this way. If I repeatedly snap hook my tee shots out of bounds, I am going to ask myself, "Why does this keep happening?" followed by, "What must I do to correct this problem?" For correction and improvement in my shot-making ability, I may need help from my golf pro. I go to him because he can identify my swing problems.

The same is true for my life behaviors and skills. I must grow. And to grow I must remain teachable and open to the instructions of my "life pro"—my Maker. I try to keep in mind that God has begun something good in me and is going to continue working with me until I understand. Because God loves me too much to leave me where I am, He will nudge me, remind me, and even keep my feet to the fire until I begin applying His teaching. The implication is clear. God desires,

---

17   Matthew 6:14–15 NLT

and more than that, He requires that I learn and grow. Otherwise, I can't move on and He can't use me for the purpose He has had for me since before the beginning of time.

Finally, I need to take God's ever-extended hand and go on with him in life's fairway.

It is very easy to focus on doing the big things right and never even consider that it is all the little things in my life picture that give it definition. It is in paying attention to the minute detail of my swing components that I generate good shots down the fairway. It is in improving the patterns of behavior in the every day business of my life that let the value and the beauty of it shine through. The beauty of golf and life with our Maker is that until my last breath He gives me the opportunity to step up to the tee and take another swing, forgiven of my past performance.

As I referenced at the end of Hole #7 the approach is straightforward. When I find myself in one of the hazards of life I need to *Grieve, Grow, and Go! (G3)*

Work for the Practice Range:

◄ Why do YOU go to the practice range?

◄ Have you hit any golf shots out of bounds or in the hazard lately? If so, what was the situation and how did you respond?

◄ Have you hit any life shots out of bounds or in the hazard lately? If so, what was the situation and how did you respond?

◄ Do you have any life shots for which you have been unable to forgive yourself and if so, what is standing in your way of self-forgiveness?

How would you score yourself in the area of **Forgiveness – moving forward**?

(Scale: Quite well ... Birdie 4; Okay ... Par 5; Needs work ... Bogey 6; A disaster ... Double Bogey 7)

Scorecard

	1	2	3	4	5	6	7	8	9	Out	Total
Par	5	4	4	3	4	4	3	5	4	36	
Yardage	547	409	320	295	363	333	278	454	378	3377	
Score											

	10	11	12	13	14	15	16	17	18	In	
Par	5	4	3	4	4	5	4	4	3	36	
Yardage	498	344	228	329	357	436	340	393	285	3210	6587
Score											

Notes:

Hole #16

Par 4

340 Yards

Perseverance

(Perseverance)

*"The continued effort to do or achieve something
despite difficulties, failure, or opposition."*

– Merriam Webster

One of the most vivid and moving exhibitions of perseverance and courage I have ever witnessed occurred during my tenure in the U.S. Navy. To be precise, the date was December 5, 1971.

It was approximately 0700 hours local time that morning. My flight crew and I were preparing to launch on the third leg of our ten-day "Cookie Flight"* mission that included stops in Guam, the Republic of the Philippines, Vietnam, Thailand, Okinawa, and Japan before returning to our home base, NAS Barbers Point, Hawaii, located on the Island of Oahu.

Ever fascinated with watching aircraft during their takeoff and landing phases, I stopped my preparations for a moment to watch as an aircraft from our sister squadron, Patrol Squadron VP 6, taxied by, fully-loaded with fuel and appropriate ordnance for a 12- to 14-hour patrol/combat mission. The Lockheed Electra, a four-engine turboprop aircraft—the size of a medium-range airliner, specially configured for Navy use—was headed to the launch end of the runway and into position for takeoff. Once in position and given permission from the control tower to proceed, the plane commander added power to the engines and the aircraft began its takeoff roll.

The plane, with engines at full throttle, moved swiftly down the runway, passing through "refusal" (abort speed) on its way to "rotation" (liftoff criteria), with all four fans doing their fair share to get the bird airborne. The nose gear lifted smoothly off the tarmac followed by the main gear seconds later in prescribed fashion. Immediately after liftoff, the landing gear was retracted and the crew proceeded with climb-out procedures.

Statements from the flight deck crew later indicated, "Within thirty seconds after liftoff, a loud 'explosion-like noise' occurred and flames could be seen streaming aft, first from engine #3. Seconds later a similar 'explosion' and flames came from engine #2, and all four TIT (Turbine Inlet Temperature) gauges were registering 'off the gauge' high temperatures (over 1200 degrees centigrade)."

Meanwhile, the flight deck crew was struggling to keep the aircraft—fully loaded to maximum takeoff weight of 135,000 pounds, including fuel tanks filled to capacity with JP5 aviation fuel for a long-range mission, and a full flight crew—aloft and maintain enough airspeed and altitude to avoid striking the surrounding hillside or worse yet plummeting into Olongapo City.

On the flight deck (cockpit), Plane Commander Lt. Mike Montgomery, Co-Pilot Lt. Brooks Mothorn, and Flight Engineer ADC Don Underwood—the three-man flight crew responsible for the safety and well-being of all concerned—were challenged with an onslaught of emergencies tumbling at them, one after another, with absolutely no idea what had gone wrong or why.

Making matters worse, due to the loss of their engines, all radio communication was lost and the hydraulic system, intended to help maneuver the flight control surfaces—flaps, rudder, landing gear, etc., was shut down due to the engine fires—making the aircraft significantly more difficult to control. (Think dramatically worse than losing the power steering on your automobile.)

To net it out, the flight deck team was faced with the loss of power, which equated to losing airspeed and altitude, all the while on a heading taking them directly over the heavily populated Olongapo City with the threat of a devastating inferno, due to the amount of aviation fuel on board, and substantial loss of life, a strong possibility.

Two issues loomed large: keep the aircraft flying long enough to make a controlled landing AND save as many lives as possible.

With the aircraft unable to maintain altitude, the flight crew made a hasty decision. The most viable option available to them was to ditch the aircraft in Subic Bay—the only flat surface available on which to land without the use of the landing gear, which had been disabled when the engines that powered the hydraulic system had to be shut down.

The pilots were able to ease the aircraft through a 230-degree turn, missing, by no more than 100 feet, one of the adjacent hilltops before coming to wings level and descending onto the bay, nose slightly up. When the aircraft came to rest, the crew scrambled through the wreckage, clear of the fuselage and into the bay, now awash in aviation fuel. Both emergency objectives had been achieved—keep the airplane flying long enough to make a controlled turn back to the water (Subic Bay) and save as many lives as possible.

Quick thinking, perseverance, and the heroic action of the flight crew protected the several thousand citizens of Olongapo City from an accident of massive proportions including untold loss of life and injuries, due to the probability of an ensuing firestorm, fueled by the full load of aviation fuel aboard the aircraft. Additionally, the lives of all the crewmembers aboard were saved ... save one.

Regrettably, one life was lost, that of Tactical Coordinator, Ensign "Ned" Cooper. During the accident, Ned's body was forced into the overhead portion of the cabin, taking his life.

The total duration of the flight was under five minutes ... five minutes of unbelievable stress and emotional pressure. The total positive impact of the actions of the flight crew that day has yet to be determined. There is one thing, however, of which I am absolutely sure. The citizens of Olongapo City are thankful, to this day, that the aircraft didn't plummet into their city.

To the three heroic members of the flight deck crew, Lt. Montgomery, Lt. Mothorn, and ADC Underwood, thank you so much for your selfless efforts and perseverance guys. You didn't give up!

As I sat recounting the events of that day in the Philippines I had to ask "Why did I feel it important to share that story with you, the reader, in what is supposedly a book about the impact of golf on my life?"

In resurrecting the story from my memory, the most cogent ingredient and overarching criteria present in the story is one of perseverance—regardless of the fact that the flight crew did not understand the "why" of the problem, they understood that they must stay in the game and play for the best possible outcome, regardless of the situation. To give up would be to lose—in this case, a life or death choice.

As I thought about the situation in which the flight crew found themselves, questions began to stir in my mind and heart.

(The aforementioned scenario challenges me to do a quick attitude check about how often I am tempted to give up on things, like a round of Golf, that absolutely pales by comparison when stacked up against the challenging scenario the flight crew described above faced.)

Where and How...?

Where and how does one learn to persevere? More importantly for me—as the father of two and the grandfather of four—where do my offspring and their offspring learn to persevere?

How does one stay tenaciously focused when data is traveling faster than the mind can think and the body can respond?

From what well does one draw the courage and clarity of thought—when all sources of dependability have momentarily disappeared—to stave off brain freeze and persevere long enough to execute whatever action is necessary?

I have come to believe that this thing called *perseverance* is absorbed more than taught. Lesson by lesson, over a period of time, through repeated practice, the function of steadfastness of purpose or conviction is assimilated and embedded into one's character.

Question: How does one facilitate the absorption and development of that character trait in the ones you love? Or, to put it more selfishly, how do I help my kids and their kids embrace the need to do what it takes to stay in the game, and strive to "get back to the water", regardless of how difficult the circumstance?

One possibility—albeit not for everyone—is "through the golf course." Golf—while one can in no way characterize it as a life or death game—is a wonderful crucible in which to blend perseverance into the character of a child.

I have loved golf from my very first round, when my dad took my three siblings and me to a local nine-hole golf course for a little Saturday together time. I didn't even know there were good and not so good ways to grip a club. Fifty plus years later, there are still many things I don't know about this ever emerging game. I am still learning and still growing.

I still love it, continue to learn from it, persevering through rounds, which at times are very "un-pretty", in an effort to continue to learn and grow. In addition, I cherish the opportunity to pass on to others what I have learned in hopes that it will enrich and enhance others Golf and Life experience as well.

"Git 'em out to Golf"

Teaching our offspring to get back to the fairway as quickly as possible is giving them a blueprint for emergency procedures that will last a lifetime. Introducing a child to the game of golf is a great way to allow them to safely develop perseverance, while they are having fun.

Golf is not an end in itself or a panacea to all of a child's challenges. It can, however, have a highly positive impact on a child's growth on the road to maturity. If a child chooses to embrace the game as their own—not just as something "my mom and dad are making me do," but also as a game they enjoy playing—something happens.

My firsthand experience is that, as they see the results of their continued practice and play, they begin to grow—not only in skill but also in their ability to think strategically through difficult situations. They also learn that to pick-up and quit is not an avenue to joy or success. The only avenue to enjoyment and satisfaction in their game is to persevere, enjoying the good moments and figuring out how to handle the not so good.

In the midst of their having fun, a switch goes on inside their being and they no longer see practice as a chore but as an avenue to success—and perseverance begins to form. A tenacity of spirit and conviction emerge that in turn provides them with opportunities. They see growth as it occurs, which stimulates more growth, and a dedication to persevere—a trait that will accompany them, through a lifetime of trials, as a welcome companion.

A side note: My mother told me I was a rambunctious, energetic little guy as a toddler. I started my quest to walk fairly early for an infant. At first, it took coaxing and coaching but quickly became an activity full of rewards. The more I practiced the stronger and more proficient I got.

This is precisely why, for a number of years I have said, "Learning to walk and learning to golf are a lot alike. To become good at either, you first have to fall and fail ... a lot." (Have you ever seen an infant able to walk the first time they tried?) The way to achieve joy and or satisfaction is to persevere—try and try again. Learn what you can and try again and again.

Golf is a wonderfully curious game. It looks so simple. What could possibly be difficult or complex about hitting a little white ball around the yard?

Try it!

I have learned that golf is a game requiring a composite group of practiced skillsets, learned over time. No one is a great golfer from day one. The more you play it, and pay attention to what the course is telling you, the more you learn. At first, it shows you its major challenges. Over time, however, you begin to recognize and develop strategies and skills to deal with the subtle nuances each situation presents. As you practice and grow in the game the more it shows you.

I love the First Tee and other junior golf programs. These programs pave the way to understanding the needs and benefits of perseverance through the safe exposure to challenging situations. The participants can play or pick up. The only way to score in the game, however, is to persevere and finish the round. The question is always before them: Do you quit—take the easy road—or do you persevere?

The youngster learns that to thrive, you must first survive. They learn that in golf, as in life, nobody promises smooth sailing. It is not a right of personhood. Sometimes the ball lands in the fairway, sometimes in the rough and sometimes out of bounds. It is dealing with these difficulties that define and refine true character and beg for perseverance.

Who knows? The real benefit to developing the trait of perseverance in your child may come into play long after they leave the nest ... perhaps on an airplane with several souls on board and things have gone wrong that they don't understand. Will they give up and say "Too hard"? Or will they persevere and attempt to achieve the best possible outcome regardless of the circumstances? The answers will lie, at least in part, in their bank account of perseverance.

Cookie Flights?

You might be asking, why were these periodic missions lovingly referred to as Cookie Flights? The answer is because in addition to delivering much-needed equipment and supplies to our forward-deployed sister squadrons, positioned in various points throughout the Vietnam War theater, they also included, as a part of their cargo, copious amounts of cookies, brownies, and an assortment of other homemade goodies as well as longed for letters from home, which were always a welcome morale boost to our guys in harm's way.

I can say, from firsthand experience, having been on the receiving end of those deliveries on multiple occasions, the goodies and letters I received from home—while deployed—were filled with much-needed love, joy, hope, and a sense of being remembered. Shortsighted as it might appear, I was much more excited to be the recipient of letters and cookies than any equipment or supplies we ever received.

I will forever be grateful for the family and friends who persevere and serve, in their own way, at home, while their loved ones are far away and still find the time to make some cookies. You'd be amazed what a cookie can do!

Work for the Practice Range:

◄ What inspires you to persevere?

◄ What are you doing to encourage or teach those you care about to persevere?

◄ What are you doing to bolster or keep strong your ability and desire to persevere?

Score yourself in each of the areas listed below on your demonstrated ability to persevere, using a scale of 1–10 (10 being outstanding).

1. Interacting lovingly and effectively with your family? ( )

2. Establishing/maintaining a satisfying social environment? ( )

3. Your intellectual endeavors? ( )

4. Your career or job responsibilities? ( )

5. Your financial challenges and obligations? ( )

6. The effective maintenance of your health? ( )

7. Following the path of your spiritual convictions? ( )

How do you celebrate when <u>YOU HAVE</u> PERSEVERED?

How would you score yourself in the area of ***Perseverance?***

(Scale: Quite well ... Birdie 3; Okay ... Par 4; Needs work ... Bogey 5; A disaster ... Double Bogey 6)

Scorecard

	1	2	3	4	5	6	7	8	9	Out	Total
Par	5	4	4	3	4	4	3	5	4	36	
Yardage	547	409	320	295	363	333	278	454	378	3366	
Score											

	10	11	12	13	14	15	16	17	18	In	
Par	5	4	3	4	4	5	4	4	3	36	
Yardage	498	344	228	329	357	436	340	393	285	3183	6549
Score											

Notes:

Hole #17

Par 4

393 Yards

A Cautionary Tale ...

(Character)

"In golf and in life, when you find yourself 'in the rough,' get back to the fairway, as quickly as possible."

– Glen Johnson

One day, while I was—atypically—deep in practice on one of the holes of my home course, a gentleman pulled up—seemingly out of nowhere—in his golf cart and stopped directly beside me. He extended a robust "hello" and said, "You look thirsty. Would you like a Pepsi?"

It was a particularly hot day with temperatures teasing the hundred-degree mark, making the offer irresistible. We exchanged introductions and he gestured for me to get into his cart, take a bottle from the cooler he had nestled beside his feet, and relax a bit while I enjoyed my drink.

He explained that he was at the course frequently and was always looking for someone to join him for a round. Then he proffered an invitation for me to join him and play a round the next day. I gladly accepted his offer and agreed to meet him the next afternoon. While I did not have a stellar round that day, I thoroughly enjoyed the time with him.

After finishing our round we adjourned to the club veranda to have a cold drink and watch others finish their rounds. It was during this time of post-game relaxation that I shared with my new friend "Harry" (not his real name) the story of my wager with my wife's son Jake—who is a very good golfer—that I would post a legitimate 82 before he would card his first verifiable 68—a wager neither of us had collected upon, at that time.

During that same chat, I mentioned to Harry that a friend of mine had suggested that I move up to one of the new high tech big drivers for greater distance off the tee. I told him that when funds were available I was going to follow through on that suggestion. He sat in silence for a few seconds and then said, "Shoot. I've got four of those drivers sitting in my basement right now and none of them is being used. In fact, I'd be glad to give you one of them. I'll bring a couple of them tomorrow, you can try them out, and choose the one you want."

Knowing the cost of the clubs to be about $400.00 per club, at that moment, I responded, somewhat incredulously, "Really?"

His response was immediate. "Yeah. I'll be here about two o'clock. You can try them and see which one fits your swing best."

True to his word, Harry showed up the next afternoon—a Saturday—drivers in hand and ready for me to give them a try. I gave both of the clubs he brought a substantial workout. I could feel the ball jump off the face of the club, my drives were sailing straight and long, some as much as 50 yards farther than I was hitting with my present driver.

After significant time of back and forth cogitation I made my choice. Harry looked on, all smiles, as I thanked him profusely for his generosity and then I stuck the new driver in my bag and prepared to leave for the day, having been there since ten o'clock in the morning.

He then suggested, "Why don't we go out on the course and give that new club a good workout?"

I demurred, sharing with him that "I have committed to attend church this evening and to play would make me late."

He responded, "Okay, but surely you can have a beverage with me before you go, can't you?"

I agreed, put my clubs in the trunk of my car, and then we then made our way to the veranda for our beverage and further conversation.

As we talked, my curiosity got the best of me, and I asked him, "How did you come to have sixteen hundred dollars worth of drivers, just sitting in your basement?"

He explained: "Well, I had just spent a whole lot of money on a new set of clubs from this particular store. When I got them out to the course and showed them to my club Pro, he noticed that my driver hadn't been properly fitted for my swing and advised that I take it back.

"When I did, the sales representative with whom I had worked was extremely apologetic. He immediately brought out four different brands of the same type of driver and suggested that I take all four of them out to the course, pick the one I liked best, and bring the rest back to him. So that's what I did. After I made my selection, I took the rest back to the shop only to find out the sales representative no longer worked there."

I then asked, "So, what did you do with the clubs then?"

To which he responded, "I just took them home and put them in my basement, and that's where they have been until today."

(At that point, because I so keenly desired a new driver, my avarice overtook common sense. I had a new driver in my trunk and a bright future of many straight and long drives ahead of me, and it had cost me nothing ... or so I thought.)

Finally, it was time for me to leave. We walked back to my car and I again apologized for not being able to join him for an afternoon round. As I was getting into my car he chuckled and said—in his raspy, basso voice—words that stung my insides like the sharp teeth of a saw blade: "That's alright, enjoy your church, just don't tell God about that driver."

We shook hands after which I closed my car door and headed out of the parking lot and onto the almost mile-long access drive leading away from the clubhouse. As my car rolled slowly down the drive I could still hear Harry laughing and saying "don't tell God about that driver."

The sinking feeling in my stomach was nauseating. I felt like I had just had a fender bender with honesty and integrity and both had come out the worse for wear. In my heart of hearts, I knew I didn't have to tell God anything. He already knew. He knew I was poised at the intersection of choice between right and wrong, integrity or something less, honesty and dishonesty, and the choices I would make were solely in my control. "82" was coming at a price much higher than I thought!

All sorts of rationalizations---Gabilicity---entered my mind. I told myself *I hadn't done anything wrong. I didn't have any part of Harry's transaction with the golf shop. I was merely the fortunate recipient of the fallout of an unfortunate situation between Harry and the golf shop. If anyone should have an honesty or integrity challenge it should be Harry, not me!*

That thinking, as erroneous as it was in retrospect, seemed to momentarily stem the tide of negative emotions I was experiencing regarding *my* involvement in the sad misadventure. It wasn't until later in the evening, while sitting in a coffee shop with my wife and a friend of ours after church, that I raised my concern to them that "I might, in effect, be in possession of stolen goods, a golf club."

I gave them some of the details and asked for their read on the situation. I might add that, for the moment, I chose not to tell them about Harry's mirthful admonition: "don't tell God."

Our friend, being an avid golfer, immediately began empathizing with me and, in his zeal to support my position, stated he "saw no problem with the situation." His rationale was "You didn't do anything wrong. You simply accepted an expression of kindness and generosity. What's wrong with that? You very possibly could offend Harry if you rebuff his kindness."

His comments were music to my ears and I turned to my wife for her thoughts. She was not nearly as effusive in her support. Her discerning nature led her to give me a non-answer saying, "I don't think it's right for me to say what you should or shouldn't do. It's up to you and your conscience."

That was not what I wanted to hear. She had placed the issue squarely back in my lap. It was at this point that I felt prompted to share the complete story, including Harry's parting comment.

When I shared Harry's caution, surprisingly, it was my wife who responded first. Without hesitation, she reached back and planted a backhand to my shoulder and said, with no small amount of chagrin, "Then you know exactly what you have to do!"

She was right, of course, but it did not make my recovery shot from the situation any easier. That night, sleep was a rare commodity. I struggled through the night, not so much with what I had to do, but how to do it. I knew I must tactfully return the club. I also knew I would need to *explain why* I felt it necessary to return the club. Finally, if at all possible, I wanted to maintain his friendship.

I spent the Sunday morning—we didn't make it to church—holding cup after cup of hot coffee, until it became too tepid to drink, and then replacing it with a fresh hot cup only to repeat the process again and again. There are many ways to procrastinate, and that morning I am sure I found most of them. I could not get comfortable with a set of words that felt appropriate to communicate my conundrum.

High noon came and went and my wife entered the living room, now in a not-so-pleasant mood; she expressed to me, in straightforward terms, that she was not at all happy with me. She readily shared her displeasure in the moment stating, "You should have known immediately what you did was wrong! Now the damage has been done. You have effectively wasted over half of a day, which was supposed to be ours, trying to rectify a situation that should never have occurred in the first place." *(Well put, if I do say so myself. – LG)*

Reluctantly, I got up off the couch, lamely apologized, and indicated that I would go to the course immediately, find Harry, and deal with the issue. So after a little fumbling around to summon my reserves, I got in the car and headed slowly to the golf course.

The moment I eased my car out of the driveway my self-talk began to rage again: *What if he was out on the course, Lord knows where, in the midst of a round with someone? What if he wouldn't listen to my explanation? What if he was offended? What if he wouldn't take the club back? What if he wasn't there? What if ... What if ... What if ...?*

Much to my surprise and consternation, just as I was making my turn onto the club drive—ironically named "Longest Drive"—I noticed Harry, turning in directly behind me, and our little two-car motorcade made the mile-long drive to the clubhouse parking lot, and I still didn't have any idea how I was going to address the situation.

Once parked, we said our hellos—all smiles—and made our ways, he to the pro shop and I to the practice putting green. My mind was racing. *Harry will join me shortly and I will need to say something, but what?*

I felt like I was talking to God at lightning speed: "You said to trust you to provide the words when the time came. That time is now! Where are they? Please help me. I want to do the right thing."

Just then Harry rolled his golf cart up to within easy conversation range, got out of the cart, and dumped about a dozen balls from his range bag onto the practice turf next to me. As he began to practice his chip shots, his first words were, "So, how's it going?"

I gulped and choked out, "Oh ... (with a silent *please God*) I have a bit of a heartache."

Harry, in his raspy voice, responded with pronounced incredulity, "Heartache? What's a heartache?"

His tone of voice insinuated a belief that "only 'sissies' have heartaches."

I took a quick deep breath, and as I did so, felt my body commence to relax as the words began to flow from my mouth, *right on time:* "Well, you were kind enough to give me that driver yesterday. My problem, after I left here to go to church, was that your words, 'don't tell God about that club', kept ringing in my ears.

"Before I go any further, I have a question for you.

"When you took those drivers back to the shop to return them and you found out the fellow who helped you out previously was no longer employed there, what kept you from just leaving the clubs on the counter and telling the sales representative to restock them?"

Harry's response was somewhat puzzling to me: "Well … just lazy, I guess."

At this point, I began to share my heart and explained: "You see, I don't go to church to 'check a box' for the week. I go because it is that point in the week when I have a chance to reflect on the previous week and reconcile my behaviors with the principles in which I strongly believe. Because the club you gave me has never been paid for, I was in the position of holding a stolen club. My conscience couldn't handle that.

"I've spent many years, in the past, ignoring my conscience and I have paid a tremendous psychological and spiritual price as a result. I don't want to go back to those days of ignorance. The price is too high.

"Because of that, I hope you won't be offended, but, I have to give the club back to you."

Harry's response was unfortunately predictable: "Well then, give it back! I don't give a @#%&! It doesn't make a difference to me!"

I reached slowly into my golf bag and pulled out the driver, respectfully handed it back to him and thanked him again for his thoughtfulness in making the offer. Thereafter we spent about an hour in uneasy general conversation as we practiced pitching and putting. Then Harry indicated he thought he'd head out to the course and "catch 18 before sunset."

I chose that point to absent myself and depart for home with a huge sense of guilt lifted from my shoulders and a peace of mind in knowing I had obeyed my Maker.

In Retrospect ...

I will candidly admit that the weekend I spent on this excursion into the deep rough of frustration caught me momentarily off guard, both emotionally and spiritually, which caused me to stray from my focus. I had convinced myself that it was of the utmost importance that I get a new driver, whatever the cost, when in fact, what I needed most was to get a new and improved swing—a process, which was making good progress before the interruption of the driver issue drew me off course.

I, in the moment, chose capitulation over conscience and character and paid a price for the choice.

I am reminded how easy it is to get unnecessarily caught in the rough of life by interruptions I could avoid, simply by staying *focused on what truly matters*. There will always be interruptions lurking in the shadows waiting to pull me—and you—off our intended course.

My challenge in any situation of this sort, where disruptions and interruptions occur, putting me in life's rough, is to *get back to the fairway of what I am trying to accomplish as quickly as possible* and move on toward the goal I am attempting to reach.

I would hasten to add that this corrective approach is not just a one-time deal. It is an imperative process that I sometimes need to implement multiple times in the same day. I find it far too easy to get caught up in the flurry of the moment and lose sight of the best course of action. I am cautioned to remain vigilant in applying this corrective process when confronted with damaging interruptions, lest I end up painfully out of bounds.

Work for the Practice Range:

◄ Have you ever been teased by your own desires to move in a direction where the "pluses" seemed to outweigh the "minuses," only to discover later that you made the wrong decision? Yes/No. If yes, describe the situation.

◄If your answer was yes to the above question, has the situation been rectified? Yes/No

◄ If rectified, what steps did you take to make things right?

◄ In addition to "don't do that again," what did you learn from your experience?

How would you score yourself in the area of ***Character?***

(Scale: Quite well ... Birdie 3; Okay ... Par 4; Needs work ... Bogey 5; A disaster ... Double Bogey 6)

Scorecard

	1	2	3	4	5	6	7	8	9	Out	Total
Par	5	4	4	3	4	4	3	5	4	36	
Yardage	547	409	320	295	363	333	278	454	378	3377	
Score											

	10	11	12	13	14	15	16	17	18	In	
Par	5	4	3	4	4	5	4	4	3	36	
Yardage	498	344	228	329	357	436	340	393	285	3210	6587
Score											

Notes:

Hole #18

Par 3

285 Yards

Beauty and the Thief ...

... Keeping Things in Perspective

(Priorities)

"The price of anything is the amount of life you exchange for it."

– Henry David Thoreau

Right now, you might be looking at the title of this chapter and thinking, "Wait ... wait ... wait! Is this some kind of fairy tale you are about to tell us?"

The answer is unequivocally NO; this is not a fairy tale! In fact, it may be one of the most difficult and painful lessons I have had to face because of my affinity for golf.

First, let's talk about the Beauty...

Those of us who love the game of golf will readily confess that the game and its surroundings provide for some of the finest metaphors of life in existence today. According to the latest data available there are roughly 14,500+ golf courses and country clubs in the United States alone and thousands more around the world, each unique with its own DNA, just as each human being is unique.

Golf is a game fraught with complexities that are both inviting and potentially frustrating. Every course is subject to its own distinct weather patterns and their variability. That weather—fair or foul—can dramatically alter on any given day the demand for player flexibility, patience, and understanding, not to mention skill. Another challenge, although not often mentioned as such, is the unmatched geographic beauty many of these venues possess that can distract the focus of even the most stalwart enthusiast.

All of these factors—physical and man-made—are bound together by a commonly accepted set of rules and prescribed behaviors, providing an unmatched opportunity to learn, grow and express our imagination and creativity through our shot selection and execution...if we are so inclined.

The beauty of the game, to me as a player, is that I am continually challenged to adjust to the never-ending and oft-times unpredictable nature of each venue and do the best I can regardless of location or complexity. When I do so (i.e., perform well) the feelings of satisfaction, pleasure, and confidence that ensue are immense.

Now comes the "Thief"...

A few years back, my wife, Suzanne, and I happened across an inspirational card from Successories, a publisher of cards with beautiful photography and inspirational comments to match. On the face of the card was an eye-catching picture of a lone little boy—probably seven or eight years old—in a red and white horizontal wide striped shirt, weathered blue jeans, and sneakers, his hands thrust in his back pockets, standing on a beach, hair tossed by the wind, staring out over an endless expanse of water.

The caption below the picture read:

PRIORITIES

A hundred years from now it will not matter what my bank account was, the sort of house I lived in, or the kind of car I drove ... but the world may be different because I was important in the life of a child.[18]

When I saw that card, and its caption, I immediately experienced an onslaught of feelings and thoughts that pierced my heart. To this day those feelings of embarrassment, remorse, and regret for the time I spent, unnecessarily, apart from my children in their formative years remain permanently lodged in my heart. Much of that time was spent on the golf course. The poignancy of my misplaced priorities and irresponsibility still linger.

(Notice the word "unnecessarily." That is the word that haunts me. The word connotes that my actions were taken voluntarily, by my choice, not some demand placed upon me. Of course, there have been unavoidable times when I have spent extended periods away from my family, due to Navy deployments abroad where no family was allowed or would have been safe.) However, there were also myriad occasions where I absented myself from my family for my own personal pursuits—golf being chief among them.)

Shortly after seeing the card referenced above, I came across a quote by Neil Portman—the first sentence in the opening paragraph of his book *The Disappearance of Childhood*—that read:

"Children are the living messages we send to a time we will not see."

These two quotes hit home with a gravity I did not expect. They pointed out to me that even though golf is a beautiful and delightful pastime, it could also be a mischievous thief of the time I could be spending with my family.

This revelation was reinforced very clearly to me, by my son—now himself the father of two—about twelve years ago when he, somewhat painfully, pointed out to me that he had intentionally put aside his golf clubs so that he could spend

18   Successories.com, LLC 2915 S. Congress Ave, Delray Beach, FL 33445

more of his free time with his kids, my grandkids. His rationale was simple and straightforward.

He said, "Dad, I still remember times, watching you pull out of the driveway and head to the golf course when I just wanted to play catch with you. You would say, 'we'll play when I get home,' but by the time you got home you were either too tired or it was time for dinner or bed or whatever. As a result, I vowed that 'when I get older I'm never going to put my kids in that position.' There will be time enough later for me to play golf, but I won't get more time to play with and love on my kids. So, the clubs are in the closet for now."

Ouch!

He wasn't being mean ... or nasty ... or vindictive. He was sharing a heartfelt conviction that he was not going to subject his kids to those same feelings—of rejection, abandonment, or second-in-line status—that he had experienced as a kid.

I never in my life, until that moment, had I ever thought of golf as a time thief. It was just a beautiful thing I loved to do and would do whenever and wherever possible. If that sounds a bit selfish and self-centered, that's because it was and is.

Please...don't get me wrong here...

I am not suggesting that I have discovered that golf is bad and I never should have started playing...quite the contrary. I have, throughout these pages, sung the praises of the game and its surroundings.

The piece I didn't learn, until late in the game, was that I must have an equitable balance between time spent on the golf course and on its trappings—equipment, practice, etc.—and quality time spent with family. It is of pivotal importance to the life of my family.

(This "aha" should not have taken 38 years ... but it did! I would like to have those years back, but I can't!)

Henceforth, I have to decide what the appropriate balance of time and energy is for me to allocate to each area of my life and which areas have greater or lesser priority.

The real question is not, "How do I find ways of getting more done in the time I have?" But rather, "What are the most important things I need to do in the precious time I have been given?" I am given only so much sand in the hourglass of my life. How I allocate and spend that time is among the most important decisions of my life.

Golf can either be a delightful component of a well-crafted, balanced life, lived for the best benefit of all, or it can be a thief that can suck the life out of the relationships I supposedly cherish. The choice and the responsibility are mine.

At this point, I can't help but recall an ancient Proverb:

"Guard your heart above all else for it determines the course of your life."

Proverbs 4:23 Holy Bible, New Living Translation

Here are a few golf-specific challenges with which I have had to wrestle:

- Do I consume seemingly every free moment thinking about my game, even though it contributes nothing to my income?

- Do I trade quality time with those I claim to love the most for more time with my buddies on the golf course?

- Does golf consume a major portion of my social conversations?

- Do I chase my passion for golf to the point of stressing my budget?

- Do I forego potentially meaningful relationships in pursuit of lower golf scores?

- Do I sometimes have a challenge discerning the difference between desires and needs when it comes to setting my priorities?

One Last Thought...

The mischievous thief I refer to in this chapter does not solely wander the landscape of golf. Maybe golf isn't your thing. It could be any number of different things or interests. The reality is that there is usually something that competes for the quality time you could be spending with your loved ones.

Take some time and identify that thing or those things you feel might be a mischievous thief. Could it be...

- Work you need to do to get ahead?

- Books you need to read or newscasts you need to watch to stay informed?

- Items such as new cars, houses, vacations, etc. that, though laudable on the surface, can subtly become necessities, perhaps requiring more income, which realistically leads to less time available for family?

- Voluntary assumption of assignments, which require extended family separations, in the name of career path requirements?

- Something else?

The list is endless and very personal. One person's desire is another person's need.

My intention in raising this caution is to encourage you, my fellow traveler in this life, to take on and *subdue the time thieves* in your life, for the good of your family. I hope we can agree that we all face struggles between need and desire. The only difference is subject matter.

You may not harbor the same interest or intensity of desire for golf that I do. I am confident, however, that you too struggle from time to time with prioritization of importance and time allocation issues. My caution is that you maintain a clear picture of whom or what the time thieves are in your life and family and do everything you can to show the thief the door.

Work for the Practice Range:

How do you derive what is an equitable balance in your allocation of time?

Suggestion:

◄ Take the time to do a rough calculation of the time you spend on weekly obligations and dedicated time:

	-- Hours--
(A) Total hours in a given week	168

Time spent per week on:

Job/Career	_____
Prepare/Get ready time	_____
In transit to and from job	_____
Social Functions, including Church, Boards, School Events	_____
Entertaining, Volunteering, etc.	_____
Quiet/Contemplative time	_____
Social Media	_____
Sleep and Rest	_____

(B) Total Dedicated or obligated time
allocations per week   _____

◄ Calculate the hours you spend overall on golf (or your thief) and associated particulars per week (in season):

Time spent watching golf (or_____) on TV per week?   _____

Time spent shopping for golf (or_____) for training, equipment, balls, gloves, apparel, tees, etc.—per week?   _____

Time spent practicing per week?   _____

Time you spend playing (including clubhouse time)   _____

Time spent in transit to and from practice and playing   _____
facilities, on a weekly basis?

(C) Rough total spent on golf (or _____) per week?   _____

(D) Remaining time available for family per week?

(A) 168 – (B) _____ – (C) _____ =   ?   _____

(E) Time available for family per day

D _____ / 7 = ?   _____

(F) One-on-one time available per family member

per day ?

E _____ / # of Loved Ones _____ =   ?   _____

Now compare your average daily per family member allocation (F) with the average daily amount of time you spend on your golf pursuits (or_____?_____ fill in the blank of other interests)

_____	_____
Hours per day on Golf (C/7)	Hours per day Per Loved One (F)

Question:

Is this sufficient quality time to spend with your loved ones? Only you can honestly answer that question. Are there any time thieves in your life, stealing your time away from what you say is most important?

(If this seems rude or harsh, you may want to assess the toll it is taking on those you say you love.)

How would you score yourself in the area of *Priorities?*

(Scale: Quite well ... Birdie 2; Okay ... Par 3; Needs work ... Bogey 4; A disaster ... Double Bogey 5)

Scorecard

	1	2	3	4	5	6	7	8	9	Out	Total
Par	5	4	4	3	4	4	3	5	4	36	
Yardage	547	409	320	295	363	333	278	454	378	3377	
Score											

	10	11	12	13	14	15	16	17	18	In	Total
Par	5	4	3	4	4	5	4	4	3	36	Score
Yardage	498	344	228	329	357	436	340	393	285	3210	6587
Score											

Notes:

On the Clubhouse Veranda…

…One Last Story Before We Go

Back in the clubhouse after the round is a very special time for me. It is a time to cap off the day, share some pleasantries, tell a few stories, and cement some relationships before heading home. I love sharing stories of the man who was my number one role model in life, my dad; one of those stories follows.

I can't play a round of golf without, at least once, thinking about him. I would like to quickly introduce him to you. He was an honorable, honest, and proud man, respected and loved by many who knew him intimately. Those who knew him well were impressed with his demeanor and his upbeat, welcoming attitude. He had a way of charming and disarming even the most skeptical stranger with his straightforward friendliness.

He would greet total strangers with almost alarming and truly memorable friendliness, reaching out with both hands, one to grasp a hand and the other to gently take hold of the elbow of the person he was greeting. His eyes would hold steady on the face of the individual as his smile warmed their soul, and his greeting, "Hello, friend," flowed like syrup over their heart.

Very few people could resist the genuineness of the friendship he offered. This approach to life netted him a tremendous array of friends and acquaintances throughout his life. His warmth and that genuine friendliness traveled with him wherever he went. He never realized that his penchant for warmth, friendship, and hospitality would be huge contributing factors to the saga of the final three months of his life.

On the evening of March 22, 2007, my wife and I boarded a flight in Chicago, bound for Phoenix and a four-day visit with Dad. While we were en route, still in the air, Dad decided that he needed to step out to the grocery store to replenish his stock of Pepsi Cola—my soft drink of choice—so that there would be plenty available.

Unfortunately, he never made it to the grocery store. He did, however, make it to the emergency room of a Scottsdale hospital in need of treatment for a serious concussion as well as broken and stressed ribs—all the result of his involvement in a three-car collision.

Many, myself included, groused to God that these highly unfortunate circumstances should not be visited on such a good man. But God knows what He knows, He has His ways, He has a plan, and He certainly does not check in with me first in the execution of His plans.

Neither does God leave His own unaccompanied, especially in the midst of their most trying times and he certainly did not leave Dad to face this last chapter of his life alone. He did, however, provide him with arguably the greatest growth opportunity of his life during those last three months.

"Opportunity..."

This last chapter proved crucial for him in his quest to get safely home to his Maker whom he had believed in and served for over seventy years. Even though Dad was highly respected and loved by many, he was not without a rough edge or two in his overall makeup and it was these particular areas that God chose to address during this final stretch.

Throughout his life, Dad had always been a quietly proud man. He had a strong sense of right and wrong, a sense of self and how a godly man should conduct himself. His heart was embossed with a strong set of views on what were and were not valid forms of worship, praise, and fellowship. His sense, of late, was that worship music had become much too loud, too repetitive, shallow, and to use his word, "vapid."

I used to gently chide him about the possibility that in God's ears there was most likely a filter allowing Him to hear precisely what the heart of the worshiper was saying regardless of type of offering, style, or volume. I dare not say he was one of the "frozen chosen." But I do think it is fair to say he lived most of his spiritual life just north of the frost line, unable to let the movements of his body and the music he projected give full voice to the joy his heart felt regarding the relationship he held near and dear with his Maker.

His behavior spoke to his quietly held belief that respect, quietude, and solemnity were more acceptable forms of worship in God's eyes than the unabated exuberance and demonstrable joy that had come to be the norm in his church of choice in recent years. His positional stoicism eventually led him to a form of spiritual isolation I believe God never intended.

He pulled away from attending the main service at his chosen church, choosing instead to attend a Bible study that dealt primarily with the historical context in which the church was born. While this did seem to satisfy his need to be in church, it did not address his need for community worship in which he so longed to take part. As a result, his spirit began to atrophy—a condition he lamented and described as the spiritual dryness of a desert experience.

"A Judgment call...pride won"

On a different front, his propensity toward pride manifested itself in a quest to maintain his mobile independence long after he had become a very real threat to himself and others. To wit, the night he drove his car for the last time—his trip, ostensibly to purchase goodies for our arrival—landed him in the hospital.

The problem with this scenario is that he had promised those who love and care deeply for him that he would not drive after dark, due to his poor eyesight. He described his seeing ability as "trying to look through the branches of a tree to see." This condition, he said, "was more prevalent after dark."

While legalistically he had not broken his promise to us—it still being early evening—he chose to go at the height of a raging thunderstorm at dusk, making it look like dark. It was a judgment call. Should he wait for my brother and his wife to come over and then have one of them take him on his errand or, better yet, just call them and ask if they would mind stopping at the store to pick up some soda on their way over that evening, or ... go himself?

For some reason, the first two options looked, in Dad's eyes, to be an inconvenience to the couple and therefore not viable, especially when he was "fully capable of driving himself."

(It is important to note here that Dad's dignity and pride were directly tied to his ability to drive and his ability to walk unassisted by any devices such as crutches, cane, walker, or wheelchair. The loss of those privileges loomed in his eyes as tantamount to the closing in on him of huge iron doors, snuffing out his independence.)

Decisions and Consequences...

The decision Dad made to go out and drive in the rainstorm set up a chain of events the likes of which he never intended and certainly would not have willingly invited upon himself. However, decisions have consequences when those decisions are put into action, and his decisions proved to be no exception.

The trip to the grocery store is a short one. But peering through the rain at dusk and trying to make the appropriate eye adjustments to effectively see through the trees, he misjudged traffic at an intersection at which he needed to make a left turn. The results were disastrous. A three-car accident ensued, the outcome of which left his car totaled and two other cars significantly damaged and Dad being carted off to the hospital. Fortunately for the others involved, he was the only one injured in the accident.

More Decisions...

After four days of post-accident monitoring of his concussion and care for his ribs, it was time for him to be released from the hospital. He was notified of this decision and asked if he wanted hospital transportation home or if he had family that would be coming to assist him. He chose to have my wife and I come and get him. In the interim, the hospital staff prepared his release papers along with prescription advice from his attending physician, which included the suggested use of a walker. This portion of his prescription was roundly rejected on the spot. *Hello, pride.*

When we arrived at the hospital and got wind of his decision to forgo the walker, I, being the one who had volunteered to bring him home, felt a need to confront this issue head-on. While we waited for the release papers to be delivered to his room, I asked him, "Hey Pop—a lifelong term of endearment from me to him—you're an intelligent man. What's up with this 'no walker' decision?" He cast his eyes downward for a moment, knowing he was on shaky intellectual ground. Then, as his pride kicked in, he brought his gaze up again and said, "I think I can overcome it."

What!!!...

I sat there for a moment with incredulity written all over my face. My insides were screaming, *What! Are you nuts?* I wanted to fly into a rant and say—in a somewhat strident voice (read yell!)—"Don't you get it, Dad? You have experienced instability in walking for the past two years. The reason you walk like a drunken sailor is that you had a small stroke at about the time of mom's passing. You have had therapy for this condition, to no avail, for two years now. What's your plan?"

Fortunately, I said none of the above and instead looked at him lovingly and pleadingly and said, "Have you ever heard the old expression, 'pride cometh before the fall'?"

"More Consequences..."

I didn't know how prophetic my question was to be. It was mid-afternoon when we arrived at his condo and had a chance to settle in after the trauma of the past four days. We were looking forward, at last, to being able to breathe and relax for the rest of our visit.

Easing the pace was exactly what Suzanne and I had come to do, four days earlier. We had made plans with Dad several weeks earlier to come down from Chicago and spend spring break with him. We had joint visions of sharing morning coffee and conversation followed by lots of rest and sunshine by the pool and dinners after sunset. In short, we were looking forward to a very relaxing visit.

The journey that followed was anything but. We could not have imagined the saga that lay ahead. At approximately four o'clock the next morning, just 14 hours after we brought Dad home from the hospital, he awoke with a need to answer nature's call. As he slipped out of bed he lost his precarious balance (no walker) and fell sideways onto the floor.

I heard the thud as he hit the floor. With that sound still fresh in my ears I bolted to my feet and ran to his side, but the damage had been done. There he lay, on the floor, unable to get up or even move to a more comfortable position. He was, as we said in my Navy days, "hard down" and in need of immediate assistance.

You would think that a man in such exquisite pain would relish getting to a hospital and finding some relief as quickly as possible. But that was not the case. Dad was more insistent that we should have coffee as we had planned and had no interest in going to the hospital. It took us two hours and multiple cups of coffee, shared on the floor, to convince him that it was in everybody's best interest to get him professionally transported to the hospital and to the help he sorely needed.

Finally, he allowed us to call the paramedics. *(It's interesting how convincing pain can be)*. It took less than thirty minutes once we arrived in the emergency room to determine that he had, in fact, broken his hip and would need hip replacement, which was scheduled for the next day.

In a matter of five days, Dad had gone from being a fully functioning individual, able to fend for himself as necessary, to losing all driving privileges and being, at best, permanently in need of walking assistance, whether it be in the form of a walker or a wheelchair. One could sense the iron doors were closing.

What's all the fuss...?

He had his surgery on schedule and tolerated the procedure surprisingly well for an 85-year-old man. He remained in the hospital two additional days post-surgery and was pronounced ready to move to rehab, meaning that he had experienced all that the hospital could do for him, under the circumstances, and it was time for him to graduate to a rehabilitation center, where the intent would be to help him relearn to walk and accommodate the new life he would be facing. He was, in the doctor's eyes, progressing ahead of schedule.

Pain management...

During his post-surgery hospitalization, and then at the rehab center, he was encouraged to participate in a process foreign to him, a process referred to as pain management. It is a process wherein it is incumbent upon the patient to tell the nursing staff when they feel in need of pain medication.

(The philosophy being that it is better to stay ahead of the pain instead of repeatedly waiting until all of the previous supply of pain suppressants have worn off before ingesting a new round and therefore going through more discomfort while waiting for the meds to kick in again.)

In addition, a patient who is not in excruciating pain is more likely to be a willing participant in some of the seemingly tortuous activities required throughout the rehab process. This practice works well and makes good sense *if* you have a cooperative patient. But the system and concept fly out the window if you have a prideful non-cooperative patient.

Dad resided firmly in category two. He could not fully accept that it was reasonable to request drugs to stay ahead of the pain. "You take drugs to deal with pain not avert it!" In fact, he had no desire to request drugs, period! Once again his belief was "I can overcome it." After several nights of fitful sleep and squirmy days, he began to get the idea that maybe there was something positive to be said about this pain management stuff (pain gets its way!).

Something is wrong...

He progressed successfully, if somewhat reluctantly, through the first three days of his intended 15–20 day stay at the center. During these three days, however, a disassociated health wrinkle began to rear its head and was fully evident by the fourth day. He had developed a stricture in his esophagus, which dramatically infringed on his ability to swallow anything, whether it be food, water, or pain meds. He could get very little down.

His nutrition supply was basically shut off and he began to dehydrate. In addition, he could not get any pain meds down. This was not good, so we requested the attention of his attending physician and were assured that the doctor would respond "shortly."

Is anybody listening...?

As minutes became an hour, and two hours became four, and four became eight with no help in sight, we began asking, "Why is nobody helping? Where is the doctor? Why don't you hook him up to a nutrient bag and a bottle of saline? What is hard about this process?" The nurses were telling us, "The doctor has been called and he says he will be in, in a couple hours."

It seems that the rehab center had no authority to provide IV therapy or any other therapy for that matter without a written prescription from the attending physician, who, for whatever reason, could not or would not make himself available.

At this point, one of the attending nurses took us aside and expressed a real concern for Dad's condition and suggested that we contact the rehab center case manager. We did and were in a face-to-face dialog with the center manager within minutes of receiving the attending nurse's advice.

(Sadly, the nurse had to ask us not to reference her in the process because of potential negative repercussions to her. To us, "Nurse Jane" was the hero of the day.)

Amazingly—see the tongue in my cheek—the case manager quickly grasped the situation and an ambulance was summoned immediately to transport Dad back to the hospital emergency room where he was immediately hooked up to IV fluids from which he took in a full liter within the first hour. (*It was at this point we chose to remove the rehab center attending physician of all further involvement with my father, stating an absolute crisis of confidence in his ability to effectively handle the situation.)*

No room...!

As life would have it, there were no hospital rooms/beds available upon Dad's arrival at the hospital and as a result, he was remanded to an emergency room "holding area" until space could be made available. During his time in the ER holding area, he was made comfortable in a private "individual litter area." The litter area was set up in such a fashion that each patient could be provided short-term care and be monitored telemetrically to track their vital signs and address any other need that might arise.

Once things had settled down a bit and Dad had received appropriate hydration and pain and sleeping medications, Dan (one of my brothers) and I left the facility, confident that the issues at hand were finally under control and looking forward to getting some rest.

Satan Comes to Call...

Somewhere around midnight in the ER holding area that evening, where everything was supposed to be safe and secure, things were about to go terribly wrong for Dad. Already fatigued from his recent surgery, the hassles of getting his body to function effectively again, and still somewhat foggy from the concussion he suffered during his auto accident, he lay on his bed now pumped up with pain medication and sleep aids in an effort to get some much-needed relief.

As he lay there on his gurney, feeling very much alone and more than a little frightened regarding what was going on within and around him, all of which was beyond his control, he watched the second hand on the clock in his cube go round and round and eventually fell into a disturbed sleep.

Quietly, and ever so stealthily, Satan seized upon this moment of Dad's vulnerability to enter his psyche in the form of a vicious and challenging dream that played out the one scenario that would frighten, sadden, and potentially defeat him spiritually. Satan took this opportunity to march before Dad's eyes and heart the lie that "The Second Coming of Christ" had occurred and that he, Dad, had missed it.

Nothing, nothing could have been more devastating to my father. He had placed his complete trust in Jesus Christ to be his Savior, and he had lived his life with the assurance that should the second coming of his Savior occur during his lifetime, he was going home, as a treasured child of the Most High God, to reside forever with his Maker. He lived with the promise he would not be left behind, and yet, encased in his dream, Satan's lie had become Dad's temporary reality.

I won't take this lying down… !

The devastation and trauma of this vision were more than Dad could handle and he was not about to just lie there and accept his fate. With total disregard for his physical condition, pain, pride, or personal modesty, he pulled free of his IV needles and slid off the foot end of his gurney to a standing position. From there he began to search up and down the hall of the ER unit for a possible door left open that would provide him access to the heaven he had been promised as his eternal home.

(It is interesting to note that he was conducting his search clad only in a pair of "fishnet" hospital briefs and a pair of protective hospital boots. In other words, he was conducting his search, for all intents and purposes, "naked." This is in stark contrast to the individual that only a few days earlier found it difficult to publicly display even a modicum of spiritual emotion. In his period of crisis, he set aside all sense of self and self-pride in his pursuit of his lifelong desire.)

The Good News…

We have no idea exactly how long Dad was left unattended to search the halls of the ER unit. But we do know that when Dan and I returned to his ER cube at about eight o'clock the next morning, we were met with a welcome gladness in Dad's eyes that I had never seen before. We were to learn later that it was only with our return to his bedside that he was able to fully release his grip on the fear-filled notion that he had missed Christ's return.

It was with great joy that Dan and I were able to share with Dad, to his profound relief, that he had not missed the Christ's return and the proof of Satan's lie resided in the fact that Dan and I were standing there in front of him. Were the "Second Coming" to have occurred, we too would have been transported to heaven, thus neither Dan nor I would have been at his bedside.

With that proof, from two people he trusted implicitly, he was finally able to relax. I can only suggest to you the release of emotions and fear along with the unbridled joy that ensued during that sharing.

Be Aware...

When I think back on that terror-filled night, which I can only share secondhand, I am cautioned by the solemn reality that Satan knows our weaknesses and our weakest points and he has no problem exploiting those to his advantage to derail the confidence and faith we hold in God's promise. *For those who believe in and follow Him, life eternal with our Maker is a promised destiny—or as the old hymn goes, a "blessed assurance."*

In the midst of Dad's frightful experience, he expressed eloquently, with behaviors he would never have considered at another time, that *nothing— neither clothing, nor pride, nor decorum, nor pain—was going to separate him from his lifelong agenda of spending eternity with God.* It was his unleashed behaviors, not his words, which were responding to the questions God asks that we all must answer, "Do you love me? Do you really love me? Are you sure?" And Dad said, "Yes! Yes! Yes!"

Moving On...

At this point, I would like to tie this story up in a tidy little bow and say "The End." But it wasn't quite the end of Dad's story. After several additional days in the hospital, he was again considered physically healthy enough to return to the rehabilitation center to continue his exercise regimen in preparation for an eventual return to his home.

His midnight experience had infused him with a newfound desire to be more outward with his inner feelings and his desire to share the love of his Maker with others. As a result, he quickly became known for his friendly and freely dispensed expression, "God bless you," to those with whom he interacted and especially to those tasked with serving his needs while a resident at the center. It is no surprise that he soon became known as "The God Bless You Man."

One Final Tug...

Even with this outward expression of divine affection, Dad was not sure he was doing all he could to express to others how completely dependent he was on his Maker. For reasons known only to him, he decided that, as he offered grace over his meals, he would raise his hands as a way to honor the King he served—remember his posture among the not quite frozen chosen? This would prove to be no easy task, his midnight experience notwithstanding. He was still flesh and blood, and old baggage dies hard.

The morning after deciding that he would offer up this gesture of divine respect, as he said grace over his meals, it was time to put his plan into action. He rolled his wheelchair to the cafeteria and was served his breakfast. As he commenced to pray, he attempted to raise his hands but they wouldn't go up—his arms and hands were not physically paralyzed, they were emotionally paralyzed. He still had just enough ego left in him to feel awkward with this outward expression of love for his God.

Unable to eat his meal due to feelings of disappointment and betrayal of his Maker, he slowly made his way back to his room. Filled with remorse, self-loathing, and sadness, he had a sense that by his failure to act on his commitment to raise his hands, he was, in fact, saying, "I am ashamed of you, God." This thought was devastating to him and he sat in his wheelchair and wept bitterly.

Later in the morning, through the din of his despair came the notion that he had another chance to express his spiritual love at the lunchtime meal. Lunchtime rolled around and so did he, to take his place at the lunch table. His meal served, he bowed his head and began to pray softly, aloud, for God's blessing on his meal. As he did so, again, he attempted to raise his hands and this time they rose to shoulder height. He concluded his expression of thankfulness with a soft "Amen."

What happened next will always be precious to me. As he began to lower his hands he heard a voice over his shoulder say "Amen."

Amen, Dad, way to go! It was as if God had said, "Well Mike, I see we've dealt with that pride thing. You've surrendered it to me. Those rough edges are gone. Well done my son, come on home."

A Final Note...

In late May of 2007, Dad slipped into a coma from which he would intermittently emerge. On the Sunday before his passing, he called and we actually had a very pleasant, though brief, conversation. The following Tuesday I received a call from his Hospice Caregiver. She indicated, "Your Dad would like to talk. He can hear you but he is unable to talk, so you share with him whatever you would like," whereupon she held the phone to his ear.

What was I to say? There seemed to be a thousand things I could say, but what did I, with all my heart, want him to know? The words that tumbled from my aching heart to his waiting ear were "Hey Dad, you know I love you, and I promise...

...I'll see you there, Dad."

The next voice I heard on the line was the caregiver saying, "He has a big smile on his face."

Mike Galley (Dad) graduated from this life into the presence of Our Maker June 6, 2007. I look forward to keeping my promise to him:

See you there, Dad. See you there.

LG

A Moment to Reflect ...

To further equip you to empathize and draw from the pages that you have read, please take a moment to reflect on your life and then briefly describe below the course that has brought you to your present position in life. Think about your family, education, social life, and spiritual background and any other factors you might feel appropriate ...

- Location born in? (Describe)

- Child/adolescent environment? (Describe)

- What was your attitude as a child? (Obedient, Rebel, Free Spirit, etc.)

- What was your spiritual persuasion during your formative years?

- Favorite activities/what consumed YOUR time as a youth or young adult?

- In the following years ...

  Formal Education – to what level? _____

  Occupation/Profession? _____

  Status? (Still working/Retired ...) _____

  Married? Y/N If yes, how long? _____

  Children? Y/N If yes, How many and ages? _____

  Grand Children? How many and ages?

- What has been the most critical setback in your adult life?

- What did you learn from that setback?

- What have you done to respond to the setback you described above?

- In light of all of the above, what is your spiritual position today? (Please circle or respond.)

    1. I have embraced the faith of my youth.
    2. I have abandoned the faith of my youth.
    3. My spiritual life has taken a different direction. (Say more ...)
    4. I'm not sure what I believe.
    5. I have no current interest in Spiritual Matters.

- What recollections would you like written about you once you have posted your final Life Score and graduated from this life to the next?

I have truly enjoyed sharing a round with you and hope we can do it again...soon.

L.G.

What's your story?

Facilitator Suggestions

- Relax, you will not be trying to "teach a class." Your function as a "Facilitator" is to help engage your group in discussion around the subject matter provided on each hole.

- To be prepared and generate the most fulfilling result, read, and encourage your participants to read through the content and questions provided on each hole in advance of your group meeting. (Remember this is an opportunity to help one another grow. It is not just a task to be performed.

- Encourage your group participants to share from their own experience. This will add individual ownership to the dialog. Remember, each individual will have their own unique "take" on what they have read and what is shared.

- Ask open-ended questions which require thought and processing, staying away as often as possible from queries which can be responded to with a simple Yes or No. You want your participants to think, share, and grow as a result of the time they spend together.

- Pick a comfortable and convenient setting for your group to relax and perhaps enjoy a snack or meal. It sets the atmosphere to enjoy a loosely guided conversation where each person feels comfortable to share and grow without judgment.

- Each participant will have his or her own thoughts. Be thoughtful, empathetic, and respectful of each individuals sharing. Remember you are all "on the grow."

- Pay attention to the body language of each individual. This will give you clues as to who might have something to share but is hesitant to speak up. (Caution: be sure your conversation/questions are not perceived as an inquisition.)

- Be sure to engage the Facilities Manager, Club Pro, or whomever by asking his or her permission to hold your sessions in their facility.

- If food and/or beverage is on the docket—which is encouraged—purchase it from the meeting facility (i.e. Clubhouse, Grill Room, Lounge, etc.). And, tip generously. This will provide additional incentive for the facilities manager to welcome your presence and provide for your space and culinary desires.

Made in the USA
Monee, IL
30 April 2022